The Churchill

First staged at the Nottingham Playhouse in May 1974, *The Churchill Play* marks an exciting new step forward in the progress of one of the most original young playwrights in Britain today. Controversial and richly theatrical, *The Churchill Play* is set in 1984. It shows a group of internees in a British concentration camp presenting a play about Winston Churchill to a visiting Parliamentary delegation.

'One of the few matters on which it is still generally assumed that there is a consensus of opinion is that in May 1940, England found a man who could and did save her. The haunting and alarming suggestion made in Mr Brenton's powerful play . . . is that the man England found was the wrong man . . . *The Churchill Play* is a work of great aesthetic and intellectual power.'
Harold Hobson, The *Sunday Times*

'*The Churchill Play* . . . establishes Brenton as a major talent.'
Michael Billington, The *Guardian*

Howard Brenton

THE CHURCHILL PLAY

*As it will be performed in the winter
of 1984 by the internees of Churchill Camp
somewhere in England*

EYRE METHUEN
LONDON

*First published 1974 by Eyre Methuen Ltd
11 New Fetter Lane, London EC4P 4EE
Copyright © 1974 by Howard Brenton
Printed in Great Britain by
Cox & Wyman Ltd, Fakenham, Norfolk*

ISBN 0 413 33380 9 (Hardback)
ISBN 0 413 33390 6 (Paperback)

In memory of G.J.

The Churchill Play was presented by The Nottingham Playhouse Company on 8 May 1974 with the following cast:

Prisoners

JOBY PEAKE	Paul Dawkins
TED BARKER	Roger Sloman
MIKE MCCULLOCH	Jonathan Pryce
JACK WILLIAMS	Colin McCormack
FURRY KEEGAN	Bill Dean
GEORGE LAMACRAFT	Bob Hescott
PETER REESE	James Warrior
JIMMY UMPLEBY	Tom Wilkinson

Guards and Wives

SERGEANT BAXTER	Dave Hill
CORPORAL TAYLOR	Eric Richard
COLONEL BALL	Ralph Nossek
MRS GLENDA BALL	Mary Sheen
CAPTAIN THOMPSON	Julian Curry
CAROLINE THOMPSON	Jane Wymark
PRIVATE	Buz Williams
PRIVATE	Stephen Chapman
ROGER	Brer

The Committee

RT. HON. JONATHAN ST. JOHN M.P.	John Joyce
RT. HON. GERALD MORN M.P.	Richard Simpson
MRS JULIA RICHMOND (A Parliamentary Private Secretary)	Louise Breslin

In The Play

WINSTON CHURCHILL	Paul Dawkins
A PRIVATE	Roger Sloman

A MARINE	Colin McCormack
AN AIRMAN	Tom Wilkinson
A SEAMAN	Jonathan Pryce
A BLACK DOG	James Warrior
A DERVISH	Bob Hescott
UNCLE ERNIE	Bill Dean
AUNTIE ANNIE	Tom Wilkinson

Directed by Richard Eyre
Designed by Hayden Griffin
Lit by Rory Dempster

Act One

A dim light. Above, a huge stained glass window of medieval knights in prayer. Below, candles round a huge catafalque, which is draped with the Union Jack. At each corner a SERVICEMAN *stands guard, head lowered in mourning. They are an Army Private, a Naval Marine, an Airman and an Ordinary Seaman. The Private is a Londoner, the Marine is Welsh, the Seaman is a Scot and the Airman is a Yorkshireman. They are young.*

A long silence.

PRIVATE (*roaring his lines. Choked, awkwardly*). Body! (*A pause.*) Body a! (*A pause.*) Body a Sir Winston! Churchill! (*A pause.*) Laid in State! (*A pause.*) West-minster Pal-ace 'All! (*A pause.*) January Nineteen-'un-dred an' Sixty-five! (*A pause.*) An' 'ere we are! (*A pause.*) Three A.M.! (*A pause.*) Filthy wevver! (*A pause.*) England! Filthy wevver! Three A.M.! Back 'ere! Inna nineteen-bloody-sixties! Be-fore Eng-land fell a-part!

A silence.

An' back dare! Be-'ind me, anme mates! Why! Wha's left a' the greatest, the biggest, blood-y most monument-al English-man that ever lived! (*A pause.*) Daddy of 'em all! (*A pause.*) An' I a poor sold-i-er! Guardin' 'is re-mains! (*A pause.*) Great 'onour! (*A pause.*) M'Mum cried when I told 'er. Loved 'im! Loved 'im, she cried. M'Mum cried. (*A pause.*) Yeah.

A wind machine blows a gust of air across the stage. A few newspapers curl in the gust. From the SAILOR *and the* MARINE *there is a flicker of ill-ease. The wind dies. A silence.*

Yeah! Somefing, somefing to write 'ome abaht! Inna years to come! (*A pause.*) Take a kiddies on m'knee! (*A pause.*) Say I was dare! . . . 'Ere! . . . Dare . . . (*A pause.*) Night they laid 'im! (*A pause.*) Dare inna dark! (*A pause. Change.*) Dyin' ferra fag.

A silence. The MARINE *coughs. A silence. He coughs. A silence. He coughs. A silence. He coughs louder, twice. A silence. A hacking, urgent cough. A silence. A louder, dry, desperate cough. He summons his saliva and leaning out, breaking the image of a serviceman at attention completely, spits. He pauses, recovering his breath, then resumes his position at attention. A silence. The wind gusts across the stage, blowing tiny little Union Jacks. The wind dies. A silence.*

So dead a' night. (*A pause.*) 'Lone wiv 'im. (*A pause.*) Wha's left of 'im. What's left a' England. (*A pause.*) An' outside the General Public. Queuin'. Dead a' night, fer th' mornin'. Right over Westminster Bridge, other side a' the river. Be in 'ere, three hours time. (*A pause.*) Coughin' all over us. (*A pause.*) Always get that. Ceremonial occasions. Sneezes an' diseases.

The MARINE *coughs. A silence. He coughs, swallows, stops the coughing fit. A silence.*

SEAMAN (*to the* AIRMAN). Eh. Mate. (*A pause.*) Eh.
AIRMAN. Shush.
SEAMAN (*a pause*). Oh my Godfather.
AIRMAN. What?
SEAMAN (*trying to look behind him, eyes flickering*). Nothing. (*A pause.*) Oh, Jesus Christ.
AIRMAN. What is 'bloody matter with ya?
SEAMAN (*a fierce whisper*). Dunye hear?
AIRMAN. 'Ear? (*A slight pause.*) Wha'?

SEAMAN. Knocking.

AIRMAN. Knockin'?

SEAMAN. Knockin'. (*Slight pause.*) Front . . . (*Jerking his head back, indicating the coffin.*)

AIRMAN. Coffin?

A silence. Dead still.

(*Scornful.*) Nuthin'.

SEAMAN. I tellye, the old bugger knocked.

AIRMAN. Ye're one under.

SEAMAN. He wants to get out.

PRIVATE. Eh, you two. Shut it.

AIRMAN. Sailor boy, heard a knock.

PRIVATE (*a slight pause*). A knock?

AIRMAN. Fromt behind.

PRIVATE. What yer tryin' to do?

SEAMAN. I tellye, there was a knock. A knocking.

AIRMAN. I tells ye, there were a knock. A knockin'.

PRIVATE. Lesall just shut it. Eh?

AIRMAN. Why? There is no N.C.O. present among us.

PRIVATE. Thassa nuff a that, you.

AIRMAN. Ha!

A silence.

Wha' can it be? Keeps us all standing here, bloody sailors and soldier boys?

PRIVATE. It's a great 'onour, so shut yer face, Jock.

SEAMAN (*at once, blithely*). A very close bosom friend a' mine, a Guardsman. Had an experience wi' a crowd a yankee school-girls while on Guard Duty at St James Palace . . .

PRIVATE. You 'eard me. You 'eard me . . .

SEAMAN. . . . Left 'im, totally exposed . . .

PRIVATE. Shut . . .

SEAMAN. To cold winds an' tourists' cameras . . .

PRIVATE. Shut up!

At once a loud knocking from inside the catafalque. The SERVICEMEN *rigid. A silence.*

A rat. Or . . . Bird caught under the (*Falters.*) lid. Lads?

A loud knocking. The catafalque trembles.

(*Cries out in panic.*) 'E can't come out!

MARINE. He'll come out, he'll come out, I do believe that of him. Capable of anything, that one. (*Fiercely.*) To bugger working people. (*He coughs. Recovers. Fiercely.*) We have never forgiven him in Wales. He sent soldiers against us, the bloody man. He sent soldiers against Welsh mining men in 1910. Three were shot. The working people of Wales know their enemies. He was our enemy. We hated his gut. The fat English upper-class gut of the man. When they had the collection, for the statue front of Parliament . . . All over Wales town and county councils would not collect. No Welsh pennies for the brutal man to stand there. In metal. (*He coughs, a bad attack.*)

The knocking from within the catafalque again.

PRIVATE. But 'e won a war. 'E did that, 'e won a war.

MARINE. People won the War. He just got pissed with Stalin . . .

CHURCHILL (*from within his coffin*). England!

The catafalque shudders.

MARINE. People won the War! (*He coughs. Doubles up. He is racked by silent coughs.*)

CHURCHILL (*from within his coffin*). England! Y' stupid old woman. Clapped out. Undeserving. Unthankful. After all I did for you. You bloody tramp!

CHURCHILL *bursts out of his coffin, swirling the Union Jack. The Churchill actor must assume an exact replica. His face is a mask. He holds an unlit cigar.*

The SERVICEMEN *turn round and back away, rifles at the ready.*

It was my birthday. The 30th of November. A dirty Autumn. Was old. Out of power. Spit on the lip. Was led to the window. Saw the English people in the street. Saw how they waved and cheered. (*Angry.*) Ingratitude! (*A slight pause. Wearily.*) The blood was denied to my brain. I sat by the fire for hours, never speaking. Set myself little feeble tasks. When did I first (*A slight pause*) see a man with a stomach wound? (*A spurt of enthusiasm.*) Cuban jungle, mah, when as a young man, barely twenty-one, so eager to see War went to Cuba, where Spaniards were killing rebels of some hue, not very successfully . . . He was, I remember, already dead when we came across him. It was a stomach wound . . . But whether a Spaniard, or a Cuban, was, was (*Falters.*) mah obscure. (*A pause. He stares out.*) Memory. Hours. (*Lowers his head. A slight pause. Raises his head.*) I went from High Office without grace. There was an Empire. Is it burnt? Drowned? Dust. Ash. Cast away. Like on the edge of some hellhole, of some mining area. Those bitter men. Today I may as well be scattered there. (*A slight pause. Then again, enthusiasm.*) Still, I can say I bludgeoned my way, through many jarring blows and shocks, bludgeoned (*With a great pout of his jaw and a gesture with his cigar hand.*) Onto . . . Mah History's stage! (*Sees the cigar isn't lit. Then to the* SAILOR.) Lad. Give us a light, lad. (*With unsuccessful jollity.*) Sailor boy!

The SAILOR *hesitates.*

(*Pathetically.*) Don't worry. On m'way to Bladon Churchyard. English graveyard. Sod. Eh? Eh? English elms. Larch. Oak. Eh? Choc-box last resting for the old man. Bloody sentimentality. Dogpiss on my grave, more like. (*To the* SAILOR, *cheerfully.*) Light! Light, lad!

A pause. Then the SAILOR *gingerly puts his rifle down. He fumbles in his pocket and takes out a lighter. He approaches* CHURCHILL. *His lighter flares.*

(*Ignores the light. Imploringly.*) Give us a kiss, Jolly Jack Tar.

COLONEL BALL (*unseen*). Sergeant Baxter.

SERGEANT (*unseen*). Suh!

BALL (*unseen*). Could we stop. Could we have light. Could we get all this out of the way please.

> *The* SEAMAN *hesitates and looks round into the darkness.* CHURCHILL *hesitates for a moment. Then leans forward and aggressively puffs on the cigar.*

SERGEANT (*unclear, then*). 'Uckin' cigar OUT! (*Unclear, then.*) 'Uckin' lights there ON!

CHURCHILL. Winnie's back! (*He makes a 'V' sign.*)

SERGEANT (*unseen*). Corporal Taylor!

CORPORAL (*unseen*). Yes, Sergeant!

SERGEANT (*unseen*). That man's cigar! (*Unclear, then.*) Anna lights!

CORPORAL (*unseen*). Yes, Sergeant!

CHURCHILL. Signal the fleet!

> CORPORAL TAYLOR, *carrying a Sten gun comes into the light.*

CORPORAL (*wearily*). Come on, Joby. Don't arse about. An' give us that.

> *Neon strip lights flicker and come on above.*

> *It's an aircraft hangar. The stained glass window is seen to be a flimsy, paper construction. There is a wind machine, an improvised thing operated by an internee –* 'FURRY' KEEGAN. *He is a gentle, middle-aged man, a Liverpudlian. He is dressed in the mixture of internee uniform and bits and pieces against the cold.*

> *There are* TWO GUARDS *at the back, very alert, with Sten guns.*

> COLONEL BALL, 60, *small and youthful for his age, though running to a little fat. He has large, soft hands, whose gestures often betray uncertainty.*

CAPTAIN THOMPSON, 29, *a florid, thick-set young man. He is an Army Doctor.* BALL *and* THOMPSON *are seen coming forward.*

PETER REESE *is to one side with a broom.*

The Churchill actor – JOBY PEAKE, *a Derby man – looks up at the lights. Vibrates his lips. He hands the cigar carefully to the* CORPORAL.

BALL *and* THOMPSON *stop coming forward,* BALL *turning from* THOMPSON *in irritation.*

JOBY *pulls off Churchill's face. His own is puckered, shifty, hangdog and sly. He is* 45.

JOBY. Give us another drag on that, lad.

CORPORAL. Shut up, Joby. You dirty 'orrible old man. An' get out a' that bloody coffin.

SERGEANT. Corporal Taylor, when you have shook this lot up you will tell me. (*He stands immobile, waiting.*)

CORPORAL. Yes, Sergeant. (*To the* PRISONERS.) Get out a that tat.

'SAILOR' (*real name* MIKE MCCULLOCH, *a bony, tough little man,* 25, *but seeming older*). D'ye like me as a poofdah actor boy, Corporal?

CORPORAL. Shut up, McCulloch.

MIKE (*adopting a mocking whine*). Sergeant, canna we change back in our huts? It's cutting cold here . . .

CORPORAL. Don't be stupid, McCulloch, don't be stupid . . .

FURRY. Do you want the wind now?

He starts the wind machine.

CORPORAL. Switch that fucker off!

FURRY. Do y' want the flags now? (*He throws handfuls of flags in the air.*)

CORPORAL. Switch . . . (*Gives up. He strides over and switches off the wind machine.*) Play's over, Furry. No more play.

FURRY. Said they wanted wind. For 'play.

CORPORAL. Are you as stupid as you say you are?

FURRY. Aye. (*Looks down then up.*) Joby said it were for wind of history. Or summat.

JOBY (*gives a wave*). Thank you. Corporal that cigar . . .

SERGEANT (*evenly*). I am waiting, Corporal. Get this rabble sorted. Then we can all go home for our tea.

CORPORAL. Sergeant! (*He looks at the cigar which he holds still, gingerly, smouldering end upwards.*)

> *The* 'PRIVATE' *laughs, then stops laughing. They are all suddenly tense. The* CORPORAL *stares, then stamps on the cigar.*

Right!

> *He realizes they are all staring at the stamped cigar on the ground. He looks at it. A pause.*

(*Gently.*) Get back in yer right togs. Get lined up, and we'll get back to 'uts.

> *The* PRIVATE *makes a farting noise. The* CORPORAL *steps smartly forward and slaps him on the face and points at him. All stock still. Then slowly they change into their prisoner clothes.*

> BALL *and* THOMPSON *in mid-argument.*

BALL. Impossible. Out of the question. To present such a spectacle to Members of Parliament? Here as a select committee officially inspecting the Camp? No.

THOMPSON. The men have worked hard preparing the entertainment for the Select Committee. It has raised morale. The costumes, the props, the words of the text . . . They have taken six months to prepare.

BALL (*shaking his head*). Not a chance.

THOMPSON. At least see the rest of the performance. This was the introduction . . . Preface.

BALL. Giant pisstake. Grow up. (*Turns away.*) Not a hope, not the sliver of a chance, Captain Thompson. More than my command's worth. Sergeant Baxter!

SERGEANT. Suh!

BALL. Have that (*Points to the catafalque, the window.*) . . . That taken away.

SERGEANT. Suh! Two men, this gear . . . Out!

> GUARDS *dismantling the catafalque and the stained glass window.*

> THOMPSON *puts his hand on* BALL's *arm, to turn him back to the argument.* BALL *stares at the hand.* THOMPSON *removes it and steps back.*

THOMPSON. Sir.

BALL. This is an Internment Camp. Not a school, for schoolboys.

THOMPSON (*tight*). I know what place this is, Sir. The men need recreation. They'll go down, otherwise. Deteriorate, already. Some have. In a few months. Keegan over there.

> BALL *turns and looks at* FURRY KEEGAN. *He is standing turned away from the others stroking a piece of fur he has taken from his pocket.*

SERGEANT (*realizes whom* COLONEL BALL *is looking at. Roars.*) That man!

KEEGAN – *Nothing.*

MIKE. Furry!

FURRY (*to himself*). Nip the wire. Wi' her little teeth. But in my pocket, quiet as a babe . . .

SERGEANT. That man, Corporal!

CORPORAL. Sergeant!

> *The* CORPORAL *rushes over to* FURRY *and swings him round into line.* FURRY *doesn't seem to understand.*

Come on Furry, cut it out.

JOBY. Bloody ferrets.

> JOBY *knocks* FURRY's *hand down, shrugs at the* CORPORAL, *does a little curtsey.*

CORPORAL. Joby . . . (*Shakes his head. He walks down the line of changing* PRISONERS, *who blow kisses to him.*) Get on, get on. (*He blows on his hands against the cold.*)

> *On the stage during* BALL's *speech . . . the* MEN *climbing into their prison clothes . . . the* SOLDIERS *smashing up the window and the catafalque . . . the huge Union Jack being lifted.*

BALL (*privately and passionately*). Doctor. (*Sarcasm.*) 'Doctor' Thompson. It is attrition. Quoting the Shorter Oxford English Dictionary at you, here. Attrition . . . A rubbing away. Wearing down. Grinding down. Excoriation. Abrasion. Or, theological . . . 'An imperfect sorrow for sin, not amounting to contrition or utter crushing, and having its motive not in love of God, but in fear of punishment.' Quote done. Doctor, this is the twenty-eighth internment camp in the British Isles.

THOMPSON. Sir . . .

BALL (*cutting him*). No, let *my* bleeding heart bleed to *you* for once, Dr Thompson. Forget that. (*He thinks. Then formally.*) No, Captain. The men may not perform this play to the Select Committee of The House of Commons on their visit to this camp.

THOMPSON. Sir, I . . .

BALL (*privately. Furious*). You what! What, you!

> *A puuse. The props are wrecked. The* PRISONERS *stand, bored, in a ragged row. A* GUARD *picks his nose and eats his snot.*

CORPORAL. Don't pick yer nose an' eat it, lad.

GUARD. Sorry, Corporal.

THOMPSON (*stiffly*). The men put the play together themselves. It is recreation. I am Recreation Officer. The Parliamentary

Committee has the brief of looking at the recreational facilities of the camp, Sir.

A pause.

BALL (*sighs*). By the authority of the Special Powers Act 1977. By the authority of the Emergency Provisions Act 1981. By the authority of the Industrial Relations Act 1981 . . . (*Sighs.*) I am not an insensitive man, Thompson. I often think will my name be blackened? Will I be blackened? At some future date. Huh? (*Change.*) Very well. We'll have your Churchill nonsense. But I have to say . . . (*Viciously.*) That you're quite a big young man, Thompson. But there's a little worm in you. (*As if he has not said that.*) But . . . Water it down, cut it about. (*Stares.*) Put a few (*Irritated gesture.*) patriotic remarks . . . About England . . . In it. That is an order.

THOMPSON. Yes, Sir.

BALL. Winston Churchill saved this country from one thousand years of barbarism. So no disrespect to the memory of that great man. (*He turns and walks the line of* PRISONERS. *Wearily.*) Yes, yes, thank you, Sergeant.

> *Before the* SERGEANT *can reply, a* YOUNG MAN, *blacked up, stands from amidst the wreckage of the catafalque. He is dressed in blood-stained rags. His left arm is fearfully wounded, hanging by a sliver of flesh. He clutches the arm. With a spine-curving twist he pulls. The wounded arm comes away in his hand. He screams.*

SERGEANT. Who are you, lad?

DERVISH. Dying wounded Dervish, Sergeant. At the Battle of Omdurman. Tenth of September 1898.

SERGEANT. Shut up! Shut up, you!

DERVISH (*at once, fast*). Strong hot wind, foul and tainted . . . The Dervish Army, slaughtered there . . . Churchill young sightseer rode across us . . . Quote . . .

> *In unison with* JOBY.

JOBY.   { Can you imagine the postures in which a man,
DERVISH.   { once created in the image of his maker, had been
twisted? Do not try, for you would ask yourself with me 'Can
I ever forget?'

The DERVISH *throws the arm at* COLONEL BALL.

BALL (*momentarily the arm is in his hands. He throws it to the
ground*). Serg . . .
SERGEANT. Suh! Corporal, that . . .
CORPORAL. { Sergeant!
SERGEANT. { Man!
CORPORAL. Douglas! Peters!
FIRST GUARD. Corporal!
SECOND GUARD. Corp!
JOBY (*casually*). End quote. (*He sniffs.*) Young Winston's early
prose. Wonderful, wonderful. Bloom of ambition upon it.

The GUARDS *coming forward.*

DERVISH. Butchery! Flies! (*Holds out his wrists for a set of hand-
cuffs wielded by one of the* GUARDS.) Under th' imperial canopy
a never settin' sun.
CORPORAL. Alright! Alright!

BALL *turns and looks at* THOMPSON.

THOMPSON. No, Sir.

BALL *goes out.*

SERGEANT. Suh!
THOMPSON (*hesitates, then*). Sergeant Baxter . . .
SERGEANT (*a little too sharp, he hates* THOMPSON). Suh!
THOMPSON. I would like to see the entertainment committee . . .
SERGEANT. Suh!
THOMPSON. . . . And anyone else, eh . . .
SERGEANT. Suh!
THOMPSON. Interested in the Churchill play, at . . .

SERGEANT. Suh!

A pause. Both men looking at each other.

THOMPSON (*stiffened*). During evening recreation. I think in the
compound. It looks it will be a fine evening, don't you think
so, Sergeant Baxter?

SERGEANT (*holds a pause as long as he dare*). Suh!

THOMPSON. Thank you.

SERGEANT. Suh!

THOMPSON. Don't harm the . . .

They're all looking at him. Pause.

Flag.

THOMPSON *goes out.* JOBY *smacks his lips, looks up to heaven, rolls
his eyes.*

SERGEANT. What do you mean by that, Peake?

JOBY. Nothin', nothin'. Just . . . (*Repeats the gesture.*)

MCCULLOCH. 'Ate 'im, dunye, Tom Baxter?

SERGEANT. Sergeant please, Mr McCulloch.

JOBY (*skittishly, to get the* SERGEANT *screwed into the chit-chat.*)
Thought y' liked cheeks o' me old arse, Sarg. Didna know
yer 'ated me.

MIKE. Don't be daft, not you. (*To the* SERGEANT.) Captain, the
boy Captain that was here just now. All rubbed up an' gleamin'.
(*Quick, sharp.*) 'Ate 'im, dunye, Tom. Man to man, get to you,
did he, Tom? Someway or other? Abuse ye? Under th' fore-
skin?

SERGEANT (*calm. They've been through this kind of exchange many
times.*) Never let go, do yer, Michael? Agitate, agitate. Worse
than a berserk washin' machine, tumble, tumble, always stuck
in there, froth an' suds flying about all over the place.

MIKE. I have my convictions.

SERGEANT. Well, yeah . . . You play with 'em, quietly. In your
corner.

MIKE. I was a union man. I had dignity. I was a union man.

SERGEANT. And what are you now, Michael?

MIKE. Now. (*A slight pause.*) A crank behind the wire. (*A slight pause.*) Sergeant.

SERGEANT. Why, so you are, Michael. (*Publicly.*) We'll 'ave all of you pickin' this stuff up an' carryin' it to the woodsheds. Where it can do fer stoves in the huts. Waste not, grieve not.

JOBY (*sadly*). True, true.

> *The* PRISONERS, *picking up debris, loading it on their backs, balancing it on their heads. The coffin is intact.*

GEORGE LAMACRAFT (*the young man who is dressed as a Dervish*). Joby, that Cap'n. What school y' reckon he went to?

FIRST GUARD. Shut up.

SECOND GUARD. Shut up.

FIRST GUARD. Shut . . .

SECOND GUARD. . . . Up.

> *They shove him.* GEORGE *gives a gasp of pain as he goes down on one knee and the handcuffs jerk.*

JOBY (*deliberately ignoring the guards' violence*). Public School.

JACK (JACK WILLIAMS, *who was the Marine*). Who are you kidding? That was a jumped up English Grammar School boy. Not the genuine thing at all. You can see the cracks round the edges if you look.

JOBY. Spot 'em can yer, Jack?

JACK. As a foreigner I'm very sensitive to the English class system.

JOBY. With a talent like that yer could set up 'booth, at a Fair Ground. Like reading lumps.

TED (TED BARKER, *who was the Private*). I'd ha' said that Captain was yer actual public school. Talks like 'es eatin' a peach.

JACK. Wetly.

JOBY. Thought Stowe m'sel. Second rate, but . . . Socially plush. I know that bilious kind of rosebud in 'is throat.

JACK (*coughs. Fights it down*). Fake. He's outright make-believe. He's got to be.

SERGEANT. Alright.

> CAPTAIN THOMPSON *walks back on. They stop and stare at him. All of the prisoners are loaded with debris. Bits of the broken knights of armour. Splinters of wood.*

THOMPSON. I apologize.

> *Stares. Embarrassment.*

THOMPSON. It's my fault. (*A pause.*) We all wanted this play. You have put yourselves into it.

> JIMMY UMPLEBY, *who played the* AIRMAN, *giggles.*

SERGEANT. Sh.

THOMPSON (*he hasn't noticed that*). I blame myself. The Colonel has made it clear that he disapproves of the, ch . . . Elements. (*Takes a deep breath.*) Of the presentation.

TED. Gotta clean it up then 'ave we, Sir.

THOMPSON. I'd like you to think of that.

> *A pause. Suddenly he realizes they are all opening their eyes at him.*

Soldiers. This makes for tensions. I would like to alleviate.

> *The* SERGEANT *seethes.*

So I would make it clear to you . . . That if I get my way, we will have a little fun with the play about Sir Winston, yet.

SERGEANT. Sure you will Suh!

THOMPSON (*Startled by that. A pause*). I thought I'd pop back to tell you that.

SERGEANT. Thank you *Suh*!

THOMPSON. I want to say. (*He fails.*) Anyway. A gesture of good faith, on *my* part. We will meet at nineteen hundred hours. (*A pause.*)

The SERGEANT *turns his head slightly and eyes him.*

We live . . .

SERGEANT. Thank you SUH!

THOMPSON. I have not finished, Sergeant.

SERGEANT. No Suh.

THOMPSON. I was going to say . . . We live in difficult times.
Times . . . (*Failing.*) Difficult for . . . (*He fails.*) All of us. (*A
slight pause. Then he turns quickly to go out.*)

TED. Sir.

THOMPSON (*stops*). Barker?

TED. Did you go to a Public School, Sir?

A slight pause.

THOMPSON. ⌠ I . . .
CORPORAL. ⌡ Shu' yer lip!

GEORGE. Fag for yer, Sir. Gotta black face here, but m'arse be
English white.

CORPORAL. Private hit that man.

The FIRST GUARD *hits* LAMACRAFT *in his stomach.*
LAMACRAFT *doubles up.*

THOMPSON. Corporal! How dare . . .

SERGEANT. Don't worry, Sir . . .

SERGEANT (*leading* THOMPSON *off*). This will be alright, Sir.
This will be nothin' 'ere, Sir. May I suggest the Sergeants'
Mess, Sir. A grog before dinner, Sir . . .

THOMPSON. Thank you, Sergeant Baxter. (*Stops dead still,
breaks away from the* SERGEANT.) Corporal Taylor.

SERGEANT. Corporal Taylor!

CORPORAL. Sergeant!

SERGEANT. Twostepsaforward!

The CORPORAL *steps forward two steps.*

Andoneandoneandoneandone.

The CORPORAL *running on the spot.*

Attention and Officer 'ere! Now!

The CORPORAL *comes to attention and salutes.*

(*Sotto to* THOMPSON.) May I suggest not in front of the internees, Sir . . .

THOMPSON (*ignores that*). Corporal Taylor, did I hear you tell this soldier to hit this man?

A pause.

CORPORAL. No, Sir.

SERGEANT (*sotto to* THOMPSON). May I suggest not in front of the internees, Sir . . .

THOMPSON (*ignores that. He's flushed*). Sergeant Baxter.

SERGEANT. Yessuh.

THOMPSON. Did I hear Corporal Taylor tell this soldier to hit this man?

SERGEANT (*sotto to* THOMPSON). Not in front of the internees . . .

THOMPSON. Sergeant Baxter did I hear Corporal Taylor tell this soldier to hit this man?

SERGEANT (*fast*). Don't know, Suh! Corporal Taylor!

CORPORAL. Yes, Sergeant!

SERGEANT. Did you order this soldier to 'it this man!

CORPORAL. No, Sergeant!

JOBY. Bubble bubble . . .

SERGEANT. Shut up Joby, no Suh! Corporal Taylor did not tell this soldier to hit this man. Suh!

THOMPSON. Sergeant Baxter! (*A pause. He controls himself.*) Did *you* hear . . . Corporal Taylor . . . Tell this soldier . . . To hit this man?

SERGEANT. No Suh! (*At once sotto.*) Best not in front of the internees, Sir. (*To the* CORPORAL.) Get these men to huts . . . All that, gear, back a' the woodsheds. (*He turns smiling to* THOMPSON.) It's like tinder, Sir. Tinder and woodshavings. I hope you will forgive me, Sir.

The men are trooping off.

MIKE. Aggro aggro.
JOBY. Lovely lovely.
CORPORAL. Be quiet . . .

    REESE *hesitates. He's upstage, in a corner.*

SERGEANT. What you up to lad?
REESE. The Corporal told me to sweep up.
SERGEANT. Then sweep up, lad. (*And personally, to* THOMPSON.) If you want, Sir, I will place myself upon a disciplinary report for this Sir.
THOMPSON. I don't know, Sergeant Baxter. I don't know at all.
SERGEANT (*quietly*). Is that a threat, Sir?
THOMPSON. Why should I have to threaten you, Sergeant Baxter?
SERGEANT (*a slight pause. Then a smile*). I'm sorry, Sir, I don't understand.
THOMPSON. I need have no fear that you may not carry out my orders. (*A slight pause.*) Need I?
SERGEANT. God forbid, Sir, if I may use the phrase. (*A slight pause.*) But . . . (*Knows he's gone too far. Bites his tongue.*)
THOMPSON. But what, Sergeant Baxter?
SERGEANT. Nothing, Sir. Ten years ago I was a lad in the Army in Ulster, did you know that, Sir?
THOMPSON (*guarded*). No. No I . . . Did not know that.
SERGEANT. Oh yes, Sir.
THOMPSON. Then you have . . . (*Slight hesitation.*)
SERGEANT (*at once*). Seen a lot of pigs stuck. In English streets, too, Sir.
THOMPSON. I'm sure.
SERGEANT. The British Army's changed a great deal in the last ten years, Sir.
THOMPSON. What do you want to say to me, Sergeant?

The prisoners are off the stage. Upstage PETER REESE *shuffles about, sweeping half-heartedly.*

SERGEANT (*a pause. The Sergeant's sickliness of manner at its most marked*). I know you're a liberal man, Sir.

THOMPSON. But?

SERGEANT. But the men think you're a (*Deliberately.*) fucking namby pamby Sunday School do-gooder fucking lily-white bleeding heart. Soft on the internees. Soldiers don't like that, Sir.

THOMPSON *opens his mouth to say something.*

(*Going on.*) And you have egged 'em on. Egged the scum on to take the piss out of a great Englishman. The soldier lads o' this camp don't take that very well, Sir. They take that, coming from you, like a cup of cold sick.

THOMPSON. Sergeant Baxter, I will have you put upon a charge.

SERGEANT. Dr Thompson, right now in this camp you could not charge your Grandma's pussycat. (*A change.*) You must know how it is, Sir . . . Men have killed officers many times over many years. Many wars, many ways. As an N.C.O. I don't like that, particularly. (*A slight pause. Gravely.*) Balmier years, quieter, milkier times I would never have spoken to an officer this way. An N.C.O. (*Sniffs, braces himself.*) Nevertheless, I do believe you ought to go and see Colonel Ball and tell the Colonel the men won't cooperate an' won't do the play. Sir.

THOMPSON. You are a conspicuous bastard, Baxter.

SERGEANT. Conspicuous, Sir?

THOMPSON. I can see you. I can see what you are.

SERGEANT (*angered*). We, the soldiers . . . Ten years o' yer own streets, yer own kith an' kin . . . But now we have become wise. The English soldier boy is getting his rocks off at last. We could run this place like sweet music. Double 'em all day, A to B, B to C an' back to A again. That's all. No plays a-bout Sir Winston Churchill. (*Change to a sweet, almost pleading tone.*)

Do drop it, Sir. You would be very popular. It's in all our interests.

THOMPSON. No.

SERGEANT. I'm sorry you take that attitude, Sir.

THOMPSON. I bet you are.

SERGEANT. I hope you don't get injured, Sir. Grenade on an exercise. At any moment a nasty moment . . .

THOMPSON (*red-faced now*). No other officer would believe the way you have spoken to me here.

SERGEANT (*blithe*). I'm pretty sure every officer has had an N.C.O. whisper in his pinky-piggy little ear'ole. One time or other. Read a lot of military 'istory do you, Sir?

THOMPSON. No.

SERGEANT. I read a lot of military 'istory. Do you know what it tells me? In medieval times before a defeated city, they cried 'avoc. And for three days the city was the common soldier's. Rape. Burn. Loot. Dance in blood, wine, stuff yerself. Disgustin', eh? Morning o' the fourth day, King'd send 'is aristocrat officers in with staves, an' dogs. Clear out the common soldier. And then send in the Archbishop, to consecrate the place . . . So the King, and his retinue, a fat ermine-robed lot, politicians all, could ride in. Unsullied. To thank God, for their delivery, and freedom. The point o' my story is . . . That the runnin' amok, the havoc, the sackin' of the city . . . Why that was the soldiers' pay. The loot and what's more . . . The ecstasy.

THOMPSON. Getting . . . (*A breath.*) . . . One's rocks off.

SERGEANT. Why yes.

THOMPSON. Dear God. In the Officers' Mess you're regarded as a fair, decent man. One of the least . . . Bull-necked of our N.C.O. strength.

SERGEANT. Then you should pay attention to what I say, you puffy ponce.

THOMPSON *a small sharp step back.*

Don't try to 'it me. I've killed men. 'Ave you killed men?
Then don't try to 'it me. (*He smiles.*) Look at it from the
soldier's point of view, Sir. 'E wants what 'e wants, bad. Do
you want what you want, bad? I mean you must do. Want
what you want, bad.

THOMPSON (*thrown*). Perhaps.

SERGEANT. . . . Less you're a real . . . Liar, I mean a real self
deceiver, eh? I mean, really washed up?

> THOMPSON *has not at all understood the passion of which
> the* SERGEANT *is speaking.*

All spent are you?

> THOMPSON *looks down embarrassed for a moment. He draws
> on military formality.*

THOMPSON. Say what you are determined to say, Sergeant.

SERGEANT (*at once picking up and parodying the manner*). Very
well, Sir. Ten years the ordinary soldier has scrubbed your
bedpan. That you may not smell the terrorist in the street.
Soldier Tom doorway to doorway, bullet in the jugular bullet
in the crotch. Ten years down Ulster then English streets.
Then the late seventies and the laws against industrial unrest.
Soldier boy at the picket line, working men 'is own kind comin'
at 'im yellin' Scab Scab. (*Scoffs.*) I went down a mine, a corporal
then, in the strike o' nineteen eighty. The miners o' that pit
tried t'kill us, y'know that? Only time I've ever been in Wales.
'Women spit very 'ard. At Corporals anyway. (*Formal again.*)
The British Army's got politicized, y'see, Sir. You should be
very glad we've not gone red.

THOMPSON. What have you gone? Black?

SERGEANT. Way o' putting it, Sir.

THOMPSON. God help us then.

SERGEANT (*Snap.*) Suh! (*Change.*) Don't push the men, sir.
Don't let this Churchill shenanigans get off the ground, Sir.
The men . . . I had to speak to you, in all fairness, Sir.

THOMPSON. I will report you, Sergeant. I will break your balls.

SERGEANT. Suh!

THOMPSON. Go away.

SERGEANT. Suh!

He marches off, strictly. A pause.

THOMPSON (*quietly, to himself*). Go away. Go away. Go away. Go away. Go away.

PETER REESE *approaches* THOMPSON *from upstage, broom in hand.*

REESE. Excuse me please. I arrived in this camp this morning. Perhaps you remember you asked me about my health, and told me I would have a medical examination later. At another date.

THOMPSON *looks at him blankly. He turns and walks about the hangar, self-obsessed.*

(*A slight pause.*) I come from a very small . . . Small place just on the outside of Aberdare. (*A slight pause.*) I was arrested this morning. But just before dawn, you see. When I arrived at work. It is a large works, anthracite smelting. Quite filthy in its way. Trees on the nearby mountainside are corroded away. Anyway. (*He swallows, a slight pause.*) I have been looking for an opportunity to speak to someone in authority. I was put in a *lorry* you see. And driven. Here, to this place. Which, I am told, is called Camp Churchill. Is that . . . Not so? (*Nothing from* THOMPSON.) In the lorry it was bad. There was an incident. We were allowed, after some time, to get out for a piss. A very bleak landscape it was. But no longer Wales. One of the men thought it was Salisbury Plain. But it was too craggy, with rock outbreaks. Perhaps it was Wiltshire? Limestone, I believe? We pissed, and there was the incident. The soldier who had charge of us was a boy, over grown men. One man, not Welsh, an Irishman, Convery his name . . . Pushed the boy. In the lorry, then in the open air . . . Ran for it. Oh, we were chained. (*Raises his wrists, looks from one to the other, a pause.*) Convery pushed the soldier lad, and the soldier lad fired. Through Convery's foot. It was so . . . Trivial. But Convery was a brave fellow. For both the soldier and the driver, also armed, were lads . . . And hysterical . . . And Convery calmed them down. Despite a wound that was ugly. Convery, he said . . . (*He hesitates.*) In any case, I had the impression he had been . . . To a camp before.

THOMPSON, *walking*.

Please, what worries me is my family.

THOMPSON *stands still*.

All I know is I am somewhere in England, I have a broom in my hand, I have been asked . . . To sweep this aircraft hangar. (*Change.*) No, that is . . . False of me. I know I am in a camp. I am detained. Please, let my family know where I am. That I'm well. I have three children. Let my wife know. Can you help me?

THOMPSON (*quietly*). Go away.

REESE. I'm sorry?

THOMPSON. Go away. Go away. Go away.

He walks off briskly, a straight back.

REESE *smashes the broom, breaks it twice, throwing the head high into the flies. It falls back onto the stage, yards upstage of him. He speaks passionately, alone in the huge aircraft hangar.*

REESE. That man with his shattered, bloody foot. Said. Degradation. That there'll be no end to it. The soldier guards they'll be like gods to us. Half a cigarette from their hands, and we'll cry with wonder, and happiness . . . Never, I said. We'll never come to that. But we will, oh we will. Read every flicker of our captors, every gesture, for meaning. Said the man with the terrible wound in his foot . . . We are going lower than the lower depths. And this is how we will survive. Leave our real selves by the gate of the camp. Like old coats. And it's not us in here, daily going lower, more terrified, more craven. We are only the hearts and livers and kidneys, the bodies of those beautiful, brave and free men. And though we do terrible things, eat each other's shit, it's not our real selves here. God knows, there's no difficulty in degrading the human animal, it's vulnerable enough. A few blows, a few weeks' starvation, a few nights without sleep. And man? Would slander a slug under a stone to call him animal. And there's no shame, Convery said. There's no shame, my comrades, there's no shame in what we will be driven to. (*He raises his arms wide. A pause. His arms flop. He sags.*) Not even the time of day. (*A gesture with his wrist.*) Had my Omega . . . (*He shrugs.*)

He goes upstage, picks up the head of the broom, comes down stage, sweeps with it as best he can.

GEORGE LAMACRAFT *is whirled across the back of the stage by the* GUARDS, *handcuffed to one. They beat him, all three men running.*

GEORGE. Canopy . . . Canopy . . . Under the British Empire's Canopy . . . Never settin' sun . . . Thick so thickly they lay . . . As t'hide the ground . . . Hid-eous cover-ing . . . decorum . . . All was filthy corruption . . .

They're off. For a few seconds REESE *sweeps alone.*

FURRY KEEGAN *comes on, surreptitiously.*

FURRY. Don't sweep tha'.
REESE. Pardon?
FURRY. Cigar.
REESE. I'm sorry?
FURRY. 'Cigar tha'. Don't sweep tha'. 'Ere, mate. (*He takes out a crumpled paper bag.*) Give us 'hand.

They pinch the crumpled leaves and put them in the paper bag.

New in, ain't yer?

REESE. Yes.

FURRY. After mess call t'neet, sidle up t'me. In compound.

REESE. Yes.

FURRY. I put on I'm a hopeless case, y'know all over 'place. Remember tha'. Treat me like I'm gone in 'ead, reet?

REESE. Right. (*Slight pause.*) My name is Peter Reese.

FURRY *ignores that.*

FURRY. I go on like I've got a ferret, in my pocket. (*He takes out the piece of fur.*) See? Like I were really 'alf cut. But I let 'em know I'm good with me 'ands. Put that together. (*He points at the wind machine. Casually.*) Learnt a trade. See, I were in their Army.

REESE. 'Their' Army?

FURRY (*looks blank*). Ruling Class.

REESE. Oh.

FURRY. Yank, that. (*The wind machine.*) Engine fan, off a Tornado.

REESE. Oh.

A pause. Then FURRY *has collected the cigar tobacco and seems about to go.*

Is there a man in here called Convery?

FURRY. Convery? Na.

REESE. We were in the same lorry. He had an injured foot. Shot.

FURRY (*shakes his head*). Na. (*Going.*) T'neet.

REESE. Yes.

FURRY. Call me Furry. 'Count a fuckin' ferrets. Okey doke?

REESE *looking away.*

Pete?

REESE. Yes.

FURRY. Toodle-oo.

He scuttles off.

REESE (*a pause. He stares out into the auditorium*). Peter Reese. Hung like an old coat on the wire. Waiting. Somewhere in England, in 1984.

A pause. The lights fade out.

Act Two

The aircraft hangar. Early evening. Through the opened doors a mackerel sky with the yellow beginning of a sunset. The camp compound. Ordered wire. The flat landscape goes for miles. English hedgerows, copses.

The lamps are not lit.

There are a few old oil drums downstage to one side. There is a pile of oil drums upstage.

A football match is in progress with old drums for goal posts. TED, JIMMY *and* JACK *are in the game.* MIKE *stands nearby, occasionally joining in. It's a free-for-all knockabout.* FURRY *is in goal.*

JACK (*scuffing hard with* TED). All they want . . . (*Scuffs.*) To humiliate us. (*Scuffs.*) Make us look daft.

JIMMY. Me! Me! Give it 'me.

JACK. Entertainment for Members of the English Parliament? That what they want us to be?

JIMMY. To me! Now!

> TED *dribbles the ball away from* JACK *who suddenly stands still.* TED *turns, ball at his feet.*

Now as I do my run in . . . (*He steps back then running toward the goal.*) Oh, 'e carves 'defence apart w'is cannonball shot.

FURRY. Don't bump inta me, I 'ate it when y'bump inta me . . .

> JIMMY *makes his dummy run.* TED *fails to pass the ball, turns round with a bit of fancy work.*

JIMMY. 'Og it, 'og it. Go on, 'og it. (*He stands and glares at* TED.)

JACK. I'm no puppet scarecrow. To be stood up before ladies and gents of the House of bloody Commons. What do they think I am? Want me to get up and do a turn 'bout Winston Churchill do they? Oh what a funny little man, they'll say. But how happy he must be, to stand up there. Jerk his arms about. He must almost like it, they'll say. And they'll think I'm being rehabilitated. Which is the word of the Government for total, abysmal humiliation. I mean what are we? Performing bears? To stand up in our chains? Our great paws held out to say . . . (*He adopts a pathetic posture, hands held out like a beggar.*) Look we're not savage after all. We're in chains. And we won't hug you to death. For we're silly bears. W' grins on our muzzles.

TED *flicks the ball up on his knee, then cradles it in the hollow of his foot.*

Recreational Activity? Rehabilitation? Winston Churchill? We should stuff the whole ragbag right up their throats. Eh, Mike?

Nothing from MIKE, *who merely puts his hands in his pockets.*

Ted?

TED (*intent on balancing the ball*). Dunno. Give it a whirl.

JACK. Don't you care? Being made mock of?

TED. I'm all for peace and quiet. And what you can get, on the side. So . . . (*Shrugs.*) Give it a whirl. See what crops up.

A slight pause. Then JACK *rushes at* TED. TED *side-steps with the ball and passes to* JIMMY.

JIMMY (*tees the ball up*). Y'ready, Furry? Fer me bone-breakin' cannonball?

FURRY. Don't kick it on me 'ead. Y'always kick it on me 'ead.

JIMMY *takes a run up.* FURRY *turns his back.* JIMMY *gently taps the ball past* FURRY.

What 'appened? What 'appened?

JACK (*sotto, bitterly, turning away*). What happened, what happened?

FURRY (*looks round*). Y' young bugger.

JIMMY. Tha's twenty-nine nil.

FURRY. But tha's only wunside, thy side. Y're not playin' agin anywun.

JIMMY. Playin' agin ye, Furry. (*He collects the ball, dribbles with it.*)

FURRY. But I ain't gorra goal t'kick inta, even.

TED *and* JIMMY *run off with the ball.*

MIKE. Difficult, eh Jack?

JACK (*spiky*). What's that?

MIKE. To keep angry.

JACK. How d'you mean?

MIKE. Keep y'bile flowing. The 'ate topped up. Keep . . . Going at the world. Eh, Jack?

JACK. I have a go, Michael. (*He coughs. A pause. He breathes deeply.*)

MIKE (*a kind of contempt*). Ay, don't you just, Jack.

JACK. We should be hard. Go at them, again and again. No respite. (*He swallows back his phlegm.*)

MIKE (*shrugs. Smiles. Spits precisely*). Ptt.

The game comes back on.

JIMMY. Leeds! Leeds! 'Appy an glorious! Leeds victorious!

TED. Rubbish.

MIKE. Halfway down the League – Division Four?

JIMMY. Yeah but they're 'ard. Y'gorra admit they are 'ard.

TED. Assassins.

JIMMY. But 'ard.

FURRY (*dodging about nervously in the goal*). Don't kick it too 'ard, I waint see it. I waint see.

JIMMY *with the ball at his insteps, looking down at it.*

TED. We gonna chuck it then? The Churchill kick.

MIKE. Y' want to do that, Ted?

TED. Look at it like this. We get up an' do a turn for these nobs . . . Well, maybe there's something in it for us.

JACK. Humiliation.

TED. I was thinking of a few crates a Guinness.

JACK. Don't let's get into booze again.

TED. No. (*Slight pause.*) Though what is very nice . . . Pint a draught Guinness . . . wi' a bottle a Barley Wine. Mixed.

MIKE. Chaser man mesel. Irish Whiskey flowin' after the cheapest bitter in the 'ouse. Very, very fast. (*Smiles at* JACK.)

TED. Yeah, but what yer *really* want from booze, speakin' personally, is the bulk and the smoothness.

FURRY. Tell y'wha'. Red wine drunk 'ard. So 'ard it 'urts. Betwixt 'alf bottles a light ale. It were 'art student, taught me t' drink like that, years ago. We drank like that all night. Then I 'it 'im, the pansy. (*Sadly.*) Still, I say this. Makes look a things very bright and shiny. Mind ye, morning after's pretty rough. Bomb damage in yer head.

JACK. Booze talk, booze talk. I'm sick of booze talk in this place.

JIMMY. Know what they're inta, over in 'ut eleven?

TED. Dressin' up as women again, are they? Got right outta 'and that did, last time. You'd go in there . . . Long Nisssn 'ut, of an evenin' . . . Fifty odd big grown men, lot a Durham lads . . . Sittin' there in frocks they'd made. I dunno. (*Shakes his head.*)

JIMMY. Na, it's electricity they're on, now.

They all look at JIMMY.

Made a resistor. Wi' wire. So to carry strength a current. Plugged the 'ole thing int' light socket. An' two terminals wi' paper clips t' put on earlobes.

FURRY. Earlobes?

JIMMY. Fromt mains. Switch 'light on, an', and ye light up, all inside. Whee. Zonk. Twinkle twinkle.

FURRY. Ay well. Takes all kinds.

TED. 'Ut eleven. Always goin' out on a limb.

JIMMY (*adolescent*). I were thinkin' of 'aving a go.

FURRY. Fryin' yer brains?

JIMMY. Why not?

FURRY (*eyes* JIMMY. *Shrugs*). Why not?

JIMMY. Ay. Why not. Neo-Luddite that'd be.

TED. You and the neo-Luddites, Leeds Chapter . . .

JIMMY. We 'ad every telephone kiosk out in a radius a twenty mile from Leeds Town Hall.

TED. Mindless.

JIMMY. Righteous.

TED. That Neo-Luddite talk . . .

JIMMY. 'Smash the World . . .'

TED. ' To make it beautiful . . . Smash the beautiful . . .'

JIMMY. 'To make it real.'

TED. Art School twaddle.

JIMMY. Yeah.

TED. Hooligan gangs.

JIMMY. Yeah, yeah . . .

TED. Smashing computers, yer dreamed of . . .

JIMMY. Let circuitry bleed.

TED. Not one computer yer ever reached. Too many guard dogs, infra ray guns and olde English barbed wire round the real hardware.

JIMMY. We brought down Post . . .

TED. Post Office Tower, oh yes. And they put it up again and clamped down on you. You were the last . . . Farts of the age of Aquarius.

JIMMY. Yeah we were stupid. Yeah we were mindless. Yeah we tore things apart just . . . For the rippin' sound. 'Long the fault lines of the world. Rip. Rip. But give us this, we really

did 'ave it in fer 'world, eh? Y'got to give us that. We really . . .
Had it in for the world.

TED (*with a shrug turning away*). You really had it in for the
world.

FURRY. Y'gonna kick that ball at me?

A slight pause. Then JIMMY *turns and kicks the ball off. He
looks at* TED. *A slight pause. Then they dash off after the ball
miles away.*

Thar they go. Lose ball, they will. Did, only a week ago.
Kicked ball over wire. An' soldier boy in 'tower shot leather t'
pieces. Like 'e were shootin' pigeon. (*Raising his hands like a
gun.*) Splat. An' leather ball . . . All shredded. On grass, 'other
side a wire.

JACK. Dream of pints. Sit in a hut done up as a woman. Reminisce
on a shot-down football.

FURRY *looking off at the game swaying a little.*

(*Shouting at* FURRY.) You are decrepit. Look at you. You are
falling apart.

FURRY (*concentrating on the game. Blandly*). Well, y'know. Y' get
by as best y' can.

JACK. Do you think that boy will really burn his brain?

MIKE. Prison talk.

The ball comes on the stage to MIKE. *He traps it, passes it t^o*
JACK. FURRY *follows the game. But* JACK *turns and boots
the ball angrily offstage.*

JACK. Hard. Hard. Go at them hard. No respite. A stone in the
mouth, spat at them. Stone in the gut, spewed out at them.

MIKE. An' tha's just prison talk. And y' know it, Jack Williams.

JOBY *enters at the back. The game between* TED *and* JIMMY
comes back on. MIKE *joins in.*

TED. Backs to the wall, boys. 'Ere comes Winston Churchill.

JOBY *gives him a V-sign.*

Really think you are 'im, don't yer, Joby. Dear oh dear. Bet you think yer standin' on the White Cliffs a Dover right now. (*The ball comes to him. He lines it up to kick at* JOBY.)

JOBY. Don't kick 'bloody thing at me.

TED. Not going to dazzle us with a bit a thigh down a right wing, then, Joby?

JOBY. Always 'ated sport. (*He sniffs.*) All them beautiful bodies. It's not 'ealthy. (*He sits down on the oil drums.*)

PETER REESE *comes on. The game being played well, seriously.*

TED (*to* PETER). Game?

PETER. Pardon?

MIKE. Get in the game?

PETER. No thank you, very much. Not just now.

TED. As yer like.

The game goes offstage. A pause. Upstage JACK WILLIAMS, *back to the audience, scuffing the ground with his foot in a corner.* FURRY *keeping goal.* JOBY *and* PETER *sitting on the oil drums.*

JOBY (*suddenly*). 'Ad y' chocolate?

PETER. Beg pardon?

JOBY. Chocolate ration.

PETER. No.

JOBY. Then you've been done.

PETER. I should have had chocolate . . .?

JOBY. Don't sneer at that.

PETER. I'm not sneering . . .

JOBY. You'll not sneer at that in a week or two.

PETER. I wasn't . . . Sneering.

JOBY. 'Ard currency, chocolate. Bar a chocolate in 'ere is worth more than the Governor of the Bank of England's own knickers . . . Signed by the Governor a 'Bank of England himself. Believe me.

PETER. Yes, I do. Of course.

JOBY. Na y'don't. Y' don't 'cos y'not felt it yet. The weight of it. That's 'ow these places, can flourish. In England. Suddenly, w' no trouble at all. Shove troublemakers behind wire. 'Cos people have not felt the weight of it. For 'emselves. (*He sniffs. A slight pause.*) Funny in't it.

PETER. Yes. What?

JOBY. 'Ow freedom goes. When did freedom go? (*Snaps his fingers.*) Thar, then, was it then? Or some ev'nin', way back in 'nineteen seventies. Wun ev'nin'. Y'were in 'pub. Or local Odeon. Or in 'bed w' your Mrs. Or watchin' telly. An' freedom went. Ay, y'look back and y'ask ... When did freedom go?

PETER. I have been given this letter form. (*He takes a buff letter form out of his pocket.*) I am told I can write one letter a month. I don't have a pencil ...

> JOBY *takes out a pencil and gives it to* PETER.

Thank you.

> PETER *doesn't write, he stares at the paper, turning it over and over.* JOBY *stares out into the auditorium.*

JOBY. What y'in 'ere for?

PETER. Conspiracy, they said.

JOBY. Conspiracy they do say, usually. (*Malevolently.*) What did y' do?

PETER. I ... Became angry.

JOBY. Ay.

PETER. I committed an act of vandalism.

JOBY. Ay. (*Eyes* PETER.) What did y'vandalize?

PETER. I would rather not say. Petty vandalism.

JOBY. Ay.

PETER. I'm ashamed. I've a wife and two children. And I've been hauled off, to this place. And I'm ashamed.

JOBY (*sniffs. Lightly*). I were a journalist, on Derby evenin'
paper. No militant, not by a million mile. (*Chuckles.*) Strike a
1980 I were a scab. Went on workin'. I were reportin' picket
line at pit gate. There were a punch-up. Like there can be, on
such occasions. When men get lathered up . . . 'Bout world,
'bout life . . . Usually is a punch-up. Anyway, upshot were I 'it
a po-liceman. Dunno why. I'm not a violent man. Summat
must a come over me.

PETER. Passion.

JOBY. What? (*Stares.*) Oh, ay. (*A slight pause.*) I 'it the policeman. And the upshot a that were . . . 'Policeman 'it me. And
the upshot a that were . . . . They did me under 'Emergency
Provisions Act. As they did us all. Ordered to be detained.
Till further notice. Four year ago, that were. (*He sniffs.*)

PETER. You've not appealed to the Home Secretary? I'm told
you can appeal to the Home Secretary.

JOBY. Na. I seen men write long letters, pour out their 'earts
t'Ome Secretary. I've 'eard men, cryin' in their sleep t'Ome
Secretary. Na. (*A malevolent glance.*) Y'not 'oardin' that
chocolate.

PETER. No.

JOBY. Fer bunce, eh?

PETER. No.

JOBY. I remember when chocolate were ten pence a bar.

PETER. More like five pound fifty now.

JOBY (*sniffs*). Inflation. In-flammation. Schubert, t'composer, died
a the clap, y'know.

PETER. I didn't know that.

JOBY. Inflames the brain. Makes artist think a weird an' wonderful tunes an' shapes. Inflation does 'same for a country. Weird
an' wonderful, till 'backbone rots. (*A slight pause.*) Anyroad,
that's my contribution t'economic theory. (*Sniffs.*)

The ball flies on. FURRY *catches it.*

FURRY. Eh, I caught 'ball. (*He squeezes it.*)

At the back of the hangar the CORPORAL *comes on. He carries a tin bath. He goes to a light fitting and switches the lamps on.*

(*Looking at the ball.*) Eh it's goin' down. Sumwun'll 'ave t'sell their arse fer 'bicycle repair kit.

JIMMY. Wha's up?

FURRY. Ball's goin' down. Eh it's all pitted.

The CORPORAL *has come downstage with the tin bath.*

CORPORAL. Joby? One bath.

JOBY. Many thanks.

CORPORAL. Won't take anythin' fer it. (*Touches his nose.*)

JOBY. I won't ask where it come from. (*Touches his nose.*)

CORPORAL. Officer's kitchens actually. They keep it 'andy fer restin' champagne bottles in ice, when they 'ave a do. *In* the Officers' Mess.

They look at the bath in wonder.

MIKE. Jesus.

TED. Pigs.

JOBY. They won't be using it fer visitin' Members a Parliament t'morrow?

CORPORAL. Spoil the 'ole image wouldn't it. Na, it's austerity kick tomorrow. Be a few cans a lager an' a slosh a medium sherry. (*Nods at the bath.*) Fer the play, eh? Bubble bath. Hurr.

FURRY. Tommy. Could y'gerr'us new ball?

CORPORAL. That will cost yer.

FURRY. 'Ow much?

CORPORAL. 'Ow about a ferret sandwich? Ferret sandwich, hurr hurr.

No one laughs.

FURRY (*seriously*). I dunno.

TED. Could do, eh . . . (*Looks round the group. Shrugs.*) Fifty Senior Service? Or cash? Forty-seven quid?

CORPORAL. I'll take the fags.

MIKE *nods.* JOBY *waves his hand.* JACK *shrugs.*

FURRY. Ay.

TED. Done.

CORPORAL. One match-play football. Wembley.

No response. He turns to go.

MIKE (*at once*). Oh Tommy.

CORPORAL. Yeah?

MIKE. Georgie.

CORPORAL. Georgie?

MIKE. Lad with the face done up black this afternoon.

CORPORAL. Oh yeah, Georgie.

MIKE. How is he gettin' along?

CORPORAL. Oh. Very . . . Very perky.

MIKE. Glad to hear of it. Where is he?

CORPORAL. Cooling.

MIKE. Under guard is he?

CORPORAL. 'E's cooling.

MIKE. Cooling off?

CORPORAL. Down. Cooling down.

MIKE. I have him on my mind, y'see, Tommy.

CORPORAL. Yeah. (*He backs away.*) One football. Match-play, Wembley football. (*He goes.*)

TED. They not dumped Georgie, 'ave they? They not dumped 'im.

A pause.

JOBY. Right. (*He takes a big lump of sheaves of paper from inside his coat pocket.*) Yalta Conference.

TED. Y'what?

JOBY. Yalta Conference. President Franklin D. Roosevelt. Churchill. Stalin. On 'shore a Black Sea. February Fourth 1945. Carved up modern world. And Roosevelt dyin'. Churchill pissed out a 'is mind. An' Joe Stalin, Joe Stalin ah ha! Sayin' nowt. (*Handing out lumps of paper.*)

TED. Joby, pages of it.

FURRY. Bloody writers, bloody forms. Sign on the line.

JOBY. It's by way a bein' a conversation piece. Churchill and Stalin. In 'bath.

TED. In the bath? Churchill and Stalin?

JACK. Oh crud, crud Joby.

JIMMY. The Dracula Brothers.

TED. In the bath. (*Shrugs. To* MIKE.) Why not?

MIKE (*shrugs*). Why not?

Laughter.

JOBY. No no, 'ang about, Lads. Bathroom a Vorotzov Palace Yalta. Eh! True story. They 'ad a palace each. Great building, great staircase from a great 'all. Winston 'ad a staff a civil servants, Foreign Office bodies, numberin' 'undred an' seventy or so. One evening, having drinks, one a civil servants said 'Wouldn't it be super . . . To have lemon in one's gin.' Next morning. In middle a great 'all a th' great Vorotzov Palace. There were a whole lemon tree planted there. In fruit. From what farm, where in Soviet Russia, 'ad it been flown at night, on Joe Stalin's order? From Golden Samarkand? From 'sweet valley a Mongolia? And all t'say to Churchill . . . (*Quietly.*) We 'ear ye. We 'ear ye. (*Loudly.*) Eh . . . Great men. Great men. (*Change.*) Right! Who's goin' t'be bar a soap?

TED. Bar of soap?

JOBY. Bar a soap. In bath. Wi' Churchill an' Stalin.

JIMMY *lies down.*

TED. This, er . . . 'Istorical fact?

JOBY. It's symbolic.

FURRY. Carbolic, more like.

TED. Oh yer.

JOBY. You be soap. (*He shoves a lump of script at* PETER REESE. PETER *recoils, staring at the papers.*)

MIKE. Symbolic a what, Joby?

PETER. Beg pardon, but I . . .

JACK. But you what?

PETER. I am not very good at reading aloud.

JACK. You can read, brother.

PETER. Not very well aloud. Not . . . Absolutely with conviction.

MIKE. What's the bath symbolic of then, eh Joby?

JOBY (*he thinks. Then he kicks the bath*). Europe. Europe, sat upon by 'bums a Super Powers.

MIKE. And the bathwater? What's the bathwater symbolical of?

JOBY (*he thinks. Then*). People a Europe! Displaced by . . .

MIKE. . . . Great bums a . . .

JOBY. Ay.

MIKE. An' soap?

JOBY. Soap? (*Sniffs. A slight pause.*) Truth.

MIKE (*groans*). Ah, come on . . .

JOBY. Bar a soap. (*Points fiercely at* PETER's *navel.*) Stands fer historical truth. In all 'er vulnerability.

PETER (*lost*). Am I to be a woman, then?

MIKE. Bar a soap . . .

JOBY (*intense*). Y'see, worn away by brutal 'ands. Now a mere slither, a pale thing. Cleansin' fragrance, floatin' away. Easily lost at bottom a bath. In danger a goin' down (*Points into bath.*) plug'ole a Fascism altogether. (*Change. Lyrically.*) Jus' a scent . . . Jus' a whiff . . . On 'dirty bath water.

TED. Oh my gawd.

JOBY (*to* PETER). Truth! I mean . . . Soap!

PETER. Pardon?

JOBY. Read.

PETER (*deeply unhappy. He reads*). I was a bar of soap, in between the thighs . . . Of Winston Churchill and Joseph Sta-lin . . .

JOBY (*interrupting*). Alright you'll do. Let's do it in 'bath. I'm Churchill a course.

TED. A course.

JOBY. Who wants t'be Joe Stalin? Sumwun 'eavy . . .

FURRY *turns to slouch off at once.*

Furry Keegan come back 'ere.

FURRY. Do I 'ave ter?

JOBY. We won't do it in 'nude fer rehearsal. (*He settles in the bath with some difficulty.*)

FURRY. In me bare pelt?

JOBY (*waves his hand about*). Add t'effect . . .

FURRY. I don't wanna be Joe Stalin in 'altogether. I don't wanna be Joe Stalin, even.

JOBY. 'Ere's ya famous droopy moustache. (*From his pocket. Hands it to* FURRY.)

FURRY. I'll jus' look after me wind machine . . .

TED. Come on Furry. Y'need a bath.

JOBY. Just you get in bath wi' Winston Churchill. (*He sighs.*)

FURRY (*climbing into the bath*). Recreational activity they call it. Gerrin' up a play. Reckon it's good fer ye. Well it's not. It's bloody murder. (*He puts the moustache on. Large, clown-like. Big black elastic band.*) Takes ye back, years. Bloody school. Bloody poetry bein' read at ye. Bloody daffodils wavin' in 'wind. An' Jesus walkin' on dark Satanic Mills. All I can remember a school. Daffodils bloody wavin', an' Jesus walkin' on bloody dark Satanic Mills. An' daring girls t'run in boys' bog.

> JIMMY *turns away and crouches down on his haunches, back to the audience.* JACK *and* TED *look at each other and shrug.* MIKE *turns aside and cleans his nails with a split match.*

JOBY. Furry.

FURRY. What?

JOBY. Shut up.

FURRY. Right.

JOBY. Just be Stalin.

FURRY. Right. (*At once to* PETER REESE, *who listens politely.*) What y'remember, all y'days? When y'were a kid. What were

all that about? An' gerrin' married. An' first kid, an' flowers in
'ospital. Wha' were all that about? Dunno. Not the faintest.
Jus . . . Sunk down. Sediment. Silt. Mud. An' world changin'.
An' money goin' mad. An' a strikes. And when Union said . . .
Leave y' back door open tonight. Fer lads t'pop in. Jus' fer
night. Y'did. I did. Left door on 'latch. Beer out. Camp bed,
eiderdown and blankets in' parlour. We 'eard 'em, down there.
One came up t'door and said thanks. Sounded a lad. Southern.
(*A pause.*)

JOBY *takes a breath.*

(*Continues oblivious.*) Indus'tr'l saboteurs, they said. Arbourin'
an' abettin', they said. Detained, they said. Why? Dunno. Put
it down t'experience, me old Dad'ld say. Daft old sod. All y'do
is . . . Get yersel a bit a cunnin' in world. What y'can. And the
rest . . . Sediment. Silt. Mud. (*A pause.*)
JOBY. Done?

FURRY *lost in reverie.* JOBY *sighs. The lamps are bright now.
The daylight has gone. Dirty rich yellow pools, shadows of light.
JIMMY springs up and kicks the oil cans that were goal posts
over. He pauses, breathing, tensing himself. Then he runs to
the back of the stage and kicks into the pile of oil drums. The
pile collapses, they bounce and spin on the stage. Then a silence.
Then he shouts from the back of the stage:*

JIMMY. Old men! Rot old men! Chop old men up! Chop up
dead old men! Chop up dead old men's England! Chop! Chop!
JACK. I agree, I say no to humiliation. I say we go down their
throats. Hard.

The CORPORAL *walks out of a shadow. A nasty silence.*

CORPORAL. Alright, gents?
MIKE. We're fine, Tommy.
CORPORAL. Oh Michael, a word.
MIKE. Sure, Tommy

CORPORAL (*falters, unable to ask for privacy. A pause*). That lad with the black face.

MIKE. Georgie.

CORPORAL. Georgie. 'E's 'urt.

MIKE. Hurt, is he.

CORPORAL. Yeah. I tell you out a friendship.

MIKE. I fully understand that Tommy.

CORPORAL. What wiv the . . . Arrangement we 'ave.

MIKE. Y'mean the stuff y'steal for us an' we pay ye for.

CORPORAL. Yeah.

MIKE. Why should that come to an end, Tommy?

CORPORAL. No reason.

MIKE. Then . . . (*He shrugs.*)

CORPORAL. Good. (*Uncertain.*) Very good then.

MIKE (*deadly*). Tommy, where is the lad?

CORPORAL. We dumped 'im, Michael.

A pause.

MIKE. That'll be the third ye've dumped this month, Tommy.

CORPORAL. The lads are very . . . Nervy. Tell yer, out a friendship.

MIKE. That's alright. (*A slight pause.*) Then.

CORPORAL. Yeah. (*He hesitates. Then goes off fast.*)

PETER (*a pause*). What's dumped? (*A pause.*) What's dumped mean?

All the others dead still. PETER looks around at them, then realizes 'dumped' means 'murdered'.

CAPTAIN THOMPSON comes on. He is out of uniform in a good sensible coat. He wears a brown felt, affectedly brimmed hat. He has a large, lovely fluffy dog with him. It wags its tail and pants eagerly. (N.B. A real dog.)

THOMPSON. Evening, lads. (*A pause.*) Take the dog for a walk. In the woods . . . And the wife, eh? (*Chuckles. Stops chuckling.*

A pause.) Well. (*A pause.*) Ah. A bath. Yalta? Churchill? Stalin? Very, eh. Yes. And. (*To* REESE.) Who are you?

JACK (*viciously*). He's the bloody soap.

THOMPSON. The soap? Oh. (*A slight pause.*) Must be off. Take the dog for a walk. And the wife . . . Good night, everyone. (*He hesitates. Then goes off quickly.*)

MIKE. We'll do Churchill for 'em tomorrow, Jack. And we will. (*A slight pause.*) To them. At them.

JACK *and* JIMMY *coming towards* MIKE.

JACK. What you got in mind, Michael?

MIKE. Breakout. (JIMMY *and* JACK *stop dead.*) Breakout.

Blackout

Act Three

A copse near the camp. Night. A dog barking. THOMPSON *and his wife,* CAROLINE. *They are shining torches at each other.*

CAROLINE. Mummy will give us money for the house, Julian. (*A slight pause.*) Julian? Say yes.

THOMPSON. I don't know, Caroline. I just don't know.

CAROLINE. It's not actually in Maidstone. More on the outskirts of Maidstone.

THOMPSON. Near your Mother.

CAROLINE. Julian, Mummy's put a deposit down.

THOMPSON. Mummy's put a deposit down.

CAROLINE. Don't be angry.

> THOMPSON *shakes his head, turns his light away. Her light plays on him anxiously.*

Don't be hurt. Don't be upset. Don't go cold on me.

THOMPSON (*upset, hurt, cold*). No.

CAROLINE (*bitterly*). I don't know why you have to feel so guilty.

THOMPSON. I don't 'Feel guilty'.

CAROLINE. You feel guilty. Because you're in the Army and because you're a doctor. In a prison camp.

THOMPSON. I do not 'Feel guilty'.

CAROLINE. Guilt. It drips off you. Like a runny nose.

THOMPSON. Alright. I feel guilty. Yes, wonderful, fine. That's me. The English leper.

CAROLINE (*irritated*). For Godsake.

THOMPSON. Unclean, unclean, along the English lanes. (*Change.*) I have to stay here, Caroline.

CAROLINE. You don't.

THOMPSON (*at once*). What's the matter with our bloody dog? (*He calls into the dark.*) Roger? Here!

CAROLINE. Roger! (*She slides the beam of the torch along the stage.*) Roger, here boy!

THOMPSON. Don't shine that at him. You know he's nervy.

The barking stops suddenly. They look at each other, momentarily startled.

(*He shrugs.*) Rabbit? Stoat trail? (*Playfully.*) Roger, all sniffy, zig-zagging along some lovely smell.

CAROLINE. Happy dogs.

THOMPSON. Happy dogs.

Both sad.

CAROLINE. I look out of the window. The window of our married quarters. At the rain. And the mud. And the huts. And the men, going from hut to hut, on the duckboards. This morning I saw a man stumble. He stumbled off the boards, into the mud. It came up to his knee. Where does the mud come from? The ever-deepening mud. And when there is a fine day the men light fires. You look across the compounds . . . And the men are stooping, by little fires . . . I've never understood why they do that. What do they have to burn? It's not only to keep warm. At the height of summer there will be little fires, the men stooped over them. It seems for miles. The prison is so strange. Another thing, why do the men stuff the windows of the huts with rags? Nail the rags over the glass, where they can. I'm so frightened. So deeply frightened of this place. I want to go back down South. I want you out of the Army and a real doctor again. Worrying about little girls' tonsils and little boys' acne. Not crucifying yourself for being half doctor, half prison guard. Tearing yourself apart. Crying in your sleep. I'm frightened, I'm sick scared. Julian? Julian? (*Nothing from* THOMPSON.) You were going to do research. Heart diseases? You loved heart diseases. You'ld talk for hours, into the night, about heart diseases. Julian?

Nothing from THOMPSON.

(*Bitterly.*) Oh, I know that silence. That stiff neck. Go on, go on . . . Flick your neck! Jerk your head, like a little boy.

A slight pause. Involuntarily, for she's caught him, he flicks his head.

That's it! The I am so innocent, sensitive and delicate gesture. (*Savagely.*) The little flick. (*A slight pause.*) Julian?

Nothing from THOMPSON.

It's not bad, what I want, is it? It's no disgrace? A house, with a garden, in the south of England. Decent. Mild. Safe. Away from this . . . Rural slum. Slum landscape, slum fen . . . Cabbage fields for miles. Derelict airfields . . . On the horizon, barbed wire . . . Men by little fires . . . (*She is near tears.*) Julian?

Nothing from THOMPSON.

No disgrace. Not wanting to be the English wife. Of the English Doctor. Of an English concentration camp.

A pause.

That's what you are, my love.

THOMPSON. I know! I know! I know that's what I am! (*A pause, then speaking fast, evenly, looking at the ground six feet before him.*) I remember, as a student. Driving in Spain. We went deep into a poor region. We drove down a track. Up over a little ridge, quickly, down into a hollow. And there before us, a gate. Wire. And in the . . . Gentle slope of the hillside . . . Holes. Sheets of corrugated iron over them. And pushing the

sheets of corrugated iron aside, and crawling out of the holes . . .
Men. Who looked grey, and like sticks. And running towards
us, soldiers, waving, shouting, 'Fuck off! Fuck off!' We tore
the car round. And drove all that day and most of the night,
out of Spain. Never in England, we said. Never in England.

A long silence.

Tell her . . .

At once, COLONEL BALL *in the dark.*

BALL. That anyone there?

THOMPSON. Thompson, Sir.

CAROLINE (*anxious*). Julian?

THOMPSON (*ignores her*). Captain and Mrs Thompson, Sir.

BALL. Ah! Walking the dog?

THOMPSON. Yes, Sir. (*He shines the light at* BALL. BALL *is in
civilian clothes.*)

BALL. Likewise. Wife and dog, eh? She's got somewhere. Wife
I mean. (*He calls out.*) Glenda? Glenda, where are you? Come
here! (*A slight pause.*) Well. (*He nods to* CAROLINE.)

Nothing from CAROLINE.

Don't want to go on about work, but the heating situation is
worrying the daylights out of me. The bloody huts should be
insulated. But then the damp's got into the concrete prefab
sections . . . It's all bloody. Chew it around from the medical
view, would you, Thompson.

THOMPSON. Yes, Sir.

CAROLINE. Julian . . .

A dog howls.

BALL. That's our Alfred.

THOMPSON. Our Roger, I think, Sir.

BALL. What good English names we have for our dogs.

The howling stops abruptly. He looks at THOMPSON, *and he
draws a pistol.*

Your light. Over there. Now.

> THOMPSON *flicks his light straight at* MRS BALL.

GLENDA (*distressed*). A young man. Over there.
THOMPSON (*to* CAROLINE). Look after her.
GLENDA. He's got black on his face.

> THOMPSON *and* BALL *run forward and find* GEORGE
> LAMACRAFT.

CAROLINE (*leading* MRS BALL *to one side*). Glenda, don't . . .
GLENDA. But he's . . . On his face.
LAMACRAFT. Did it to me. Behind a woodshed thurr . . . Then
dumped me in the dustbin, an' took me out. Wi' the refuse,
come nightfall.
THOMPSON. Who? Who did?
LAMACRAFT. Be fool t'say, wouldn't I.
THOMPSON (*to* BALL). I know him. Hut nine. George Lama-
craft.
LAMACRAFT. Doctor Thompson.
THOMPSON (*lifts him round the shoulders*). Yes, George. What?
LAMACRAFT. Killed your dog, Doctor.

> THOMPSON *looks away and sees the dog.* BALL *goes and picks*
> *the dog up, then throws it down in disgust.*

Poor savage. Eh? Eh? English soldiers? Poor savage Dervish,
lover of God. (*Pain.*) Dyin' in a sand. One a Winston's Wars
weren't it, when he was a young man. Young blood. Inna sand.
(*He lifts himself a little.*) Can you imagine the postures in
which a man . . . (*He dies.*)

> *A pause. The actors switch their lamps out.*

Act Four

The aircraft hangar. The doors are open. Bright, afternoon sunlight. In the hangar a stage has been erected. It has a Union Jack curtain. Comfortable chairs are set before it. Its crude lighting rig is in sight with a lighting board to one side. FURRY *sits by it, carefully smoking a butt.*

A raucous version of 'Puppet On A String' by a brassband is being played over the loudspeakers. Outside the doors a helicopter lands. A blast of air across the aircraft hangar rocks the little stage. FURRY, *unconcerned, shelters his cigarette.*

The blast dies down. FURRY *stubs his cigarette out. The* SELECT COMMITTEE, COLONEL *and* MRS BALL, CAPTAIN *and* MRS THOMPSON, SERGEANT BAXTER *and* CORPORAL TAYLOR *come on. The* SELECT COMMITTEE, MR JONATHAN ST. JOHN (*Con-Lab. Ruling 'National Government' Coalition*) *and* MR GERALD MORN (*Soc. Lab.*) *They are accompanied by* MRS JULIA RICHMOND, *a young civil service secretary to the Committee. They are all very well dressed, the camel hair, the silvery suit,* MRS RICHMOND's *pastel-shaded suit, coat and hat. They sweep on to before the stage. From across the hangar a* SOLDIER *approaches with a tray of drinks. A* PRIVATE *closes the door of the hangar. The music on the loudspeakers stops. Everyone is smiling.*

BALL. Sherry?

> *They all take a glass, politely. Not the* SERGEANT *and the* CORPORAL.

Ladies and Gentlemen. The Queen.

SERGEANT. Shun an' salute!

The SERGEANT, *the* CORPORAL *and the* PRIVATE, *tray to one side in his left hand, come to attention and salute.*

ALL. The Queen/Queen/Queen.

They all drain the sherry glasses. A pause. A moment's hiatus. Then they all put the drinks back on the tray.

ST. JOHN. I am Jonathan St. John, Chairman of this Sub-Committee of the Committee of Ways and Means.

BALL (*salutes*). Sir.

THOMPSON *salutes.*

ST. JOHN. This is the Right Honourable Mr Gerald Morn of the Socialist Labour Opposition. He is Vice-Chairman of the Committee.

MORN. How do you do.

BALL (*salutes*). Sir.

ST. JOHN. This is Mrs Julia Richmond, our Civil Service Secretary. On loan from the Min. of Defence Think Tank.

JULIA. How do you do.

BALL (*salutes*). Ma'am.

JULIA. Captain. (*She offers her hand.*)

THOMPSON (*shakes hands with her and salutes*). Ma'am.

ST. JOHN. As Chairman of the Committee I am, of course, of the Party of the Government of the Day. But, since that Party is a coalition of the Conservative Party and part of the Labour Party . . . Not the part to which Mr Morn still stubbornly adheres to . . .

MORN *gives a little wave. Polite titters.*

Since we have a Con-Lab. Government, I think it only right to tell you I am more Con. than Lab. Very much more.

Polite titters.

BALL. On behalf of the Officers, other ranks and men, and the detainees, I am very pleased to welcome you to Churchill. This is Captain Thompson, our Medical Officer and Recreational Duties Officer, responsible for the prisoners' bodily and psychological welfare.

THOMPSON (*salutes and shakes hands with* ST. JOHN *and* MORN. *Turns to* JULIA). Ah . . .

She smiles, shrugs. They shake hands again. He salutes. A difficult pause.

GLENDA. Perhaps we could all now . . . (*She looks at* BALL.)

BALL. Oh yes. This is my wife.

ST. JOHN. How do you do. (*Shakes.*)

GLENDA. Very well, thank you.

JULIA (*shakes*). How do you do.

GLENDA. Very well, thank you.

MORN (*shakes*). How do you do?

GLENDA. Very well, thank you.

THOMPSON. This is my wife, Caroline.

ST. JOHN (*shakes*). How do you do.

CAROLINE. Very well, thank you.

JULIA (*shakes*). How do you do.

GLENDA. Philip?

BALL. What?

GLENDA. The . . .

BALL. What? Oh . . . (*Turning to the* SERGEANT.)

The SERGEANT *whispers to the* PRIVATE.

PRIVATE. Right, Sergeant. (*He goes off.*)

BALL (*edgily*). More drink, Sergeant Baxter.

SERGEANT. On its way, Sir.

GLENDA. If, during your inspection time here you are at any time dirty . . . And would like a shower, or bath, you are very welcome to use our bathroom. (*She smiles at* JULIA.)

JULIA (*unsmiling*). Thank you.

They are all looking at BALL. *A pause.*

BALL (*creases a smile*). As the Committee you are welcome to inspect what you will. However, I would ask you to remain accompanied by an N.C.O. Sergeant Baxter here has detailed a rota of the Sergeants' Mess to accompany you.

MORN. 'Accompany?'

ST. JOHN. I'm sure that . . .

BALL (*interrupting*). If . . . (*A slight pause.*) I'm sorry, Sir, I interrupted you.

ST. JOHN. No, not at all. You were going to say, Colonel?

BALL. Merely if you would please be accompanied, we would be grateful. We think it would be best, and . . . We would like to insist.

MORN. Would you, Colonel.

ST. JOHN. I was going to say we do not know the moods, the ins and outs, ups and downs . . . Of the camp. A body of men is continually changing, day to day. And, I'm sure, that we should accept very good advice.

MORN. Then we are not to see any internee alone. I don't think that's good. I don't think that is good at all. I think it only right we speak to the prisoners . . . The 'Detainees' . . . Alone.

BALL. If . . .

ST. JOHN (*interrupting*). I'm sure . . .

A slight pause.

BALL. Sorry, Sir.

ST. JOHN. No, not at all. You were going to say, Colonel?

BALL. We live under great pressure, Sir. Boiling pressure. You are quite right to speak of a 'Body of Men.' A body of men has its own passions. Pathos. Sense of humour, sense of outrage. The men do not see themselves as criminals. Society may see them as such. They are detained under a lawful act of Parliament. But they do not see themselves as prisoners, gaoled. This makes them at once arrogant, and prone to crises of morale.

MORN. You mean they despair.

BALL (*deadpan*). Sir?

JULIA (*to* THOMPSON, *suddenly*). You regard recreation as therapeutic?

THOMPSON. You do not.

JULIA. It provides an environment for conspiracy. Also solidarity between internees.

THOMPSON. You would prefer them in chicken coops.

JULIA. I would prefer them to be controlled.

THOMPSON. I've heard of your theory, Mrs Richmond. The white box?

GLENDA. The white box, what is that?

THOMPSON. Treatment for insurgents.

GLENDA. Yes?

JULIA. Sensory withdrawal.

THOMPSON. You are tied in a white room. The eye cannot focus. The white, it is an ionized paint?

JULIA *nods.*

Is infinite. Like the dark sky of a moonless night. Infinite. But white. And in the end you become a white, three-D void. Of course, there are drugs. And surgery.

JULIA. To implant electrode controls . . .

THOMPSON. You cut the brain.

GLENDA (*a slight pause*). Yes?

JULIA. It is still a Min. of Defence study paper.

THOMPSON. And butchery.

JULIA. Yes. But against the butchers. (THOMPSON *stunned.*)

GLENDA. Yes . . .

BALL. If . . .

ST. JOHN (*interrupting*). I'm sure.

Both glare at each other. A pause.

BALL. Sorry, Sir.

ST. JOHN (*recovers completely*). No, not at all. You were going to say, Colonel?

BALL. If . . . A more appropriate time could be found. For a wide-ranging discussion, in depth. (*He waves at the little stage.*) The men have prepared an entertainment, in the nature of something like a play. Since your Committee's terms of reference are to look at the welfare of detainees . . . This may be of interest to you.

MORN *looks pissed off.*

(*Ploughs on.*) The aircraft hangar here, we use as a recreation and assembly area. In itself, it's something of a marvel of a building. Second World War. And way back there in the early nineteen forties, very hush hush. Frank Whittle's early, first jet engine was test flown here. Two of 'em . . . Slung under the wings of a Wellington Bomber. A great secret, over the villages. How many land-girls looked up and saw the impossible in the sky? But no one said a word. Shall we sit on the chairs?

MORN (*at once*). As I see it . . . AND I don't see why we should not go hammer and tongs at this from the start . . . This Committee is a dead alley-cat. (*Louder.*) Dead alley-cat, stomach well on the rot.

ST. JOHN. Don't be so lurid, Gerald.

MORN. No one wants us. We're slung from garden to garden. A dead alley-cat.

ST. JOHN. Need we air this? We have aired this, again and again.

MORN (*ignores that*). Colonel, this Committee is hamstrung. All we are allowed to do, by the terms of reference haggled over . . . And, God knows, haggled over long enough . . . Is to look into the finances of this camp. Not should we spend money on barbed wire . . . But are we buying the cheapest barbed wire. Savvey?

BALL (*neutral*). Sir.

MORN. My Party has stretched the terms of our inspection here

to include the welfare of the detainees. Health and recreation.
See how pink their tongues are, how free the backs of their
necks are from boils. And are they screaming or not. And are
there enough footballs and cricket pads for the inmates of the
English Dachau.

ST. JOHN. Oh God.

BALL (*out of the blue*). You oppose internment, Sir?

> *A pause. All dead still.* FURRY *looking down at the floor. He
> sees the butt he trod out. He stoops and picks it up. Stares at it.
> Sniffs it. He looks up straight at the* SERGEANT.

SERGEANT (*sotto*). Don't do that, don't you do that, don't do
that.

FURRY (*loudly*). Me butt. (*He puts the butt behind his ear.*)

MORN. And you, Colonel. (*A slight pause.*)

COLONEL. Me, Mr Morn? (*A slight pause.*) Sir?

MORN. You. (*Deadly.*) What about you, are you for or against
shoving your social enemies into Internment Camps without
trial?

COLONEL. I'm a soldier. Sir.

MORN. But are you happy in your work?

> FURRY *takes the butt from behind his ear and fiddles with it.
> The* SERGEANT *loses patience and strides over, slaps the butt
> out of* FURRY's *hand.*

SERGEANT (*sotto*). Don't you, don't you, don't you . . . Do that.

FURRY (*loudly*). Me butt.

> *All looking at the* SERGEANT.

SERGEANT (*embarrassed*). Detainee. Fiddling, Suh! Fiddlin' with
a cigarette butt, Suh! Very un'ealthy 'abit, Suh! Pick anythin'
up off the floor they would, Suh!

BALL. Yes. Thank you, Sergeant.

SERGEANT. Suh.

BALL (*to* MORN). No soldier likes internal security. Like putting your own language up against the wall. Bearing a bayonet down your own streets. Barbed wire in your own fields and woods. There is a heartbreak about it.

MORN. Kith and kin.

BALL. That, Sir.

MORN. Don't grimace, Colonel.

BALL. Mr Morn?

MORN (*he steps close to* BALL. *Their noses are nearly touching*). You grimaced.

ST. JOHN. Gerald, please. Your flair for the eye-ball to eye-ball confrontation can escalate into grotesque bad taste. So please stop it.

MORN. Sod off. I'm enjoying myself. And . . . I have a question of Colonel Ball. My question is a personal one. (*A slight pause. Quietly.*) Have you an itch, Colonel Ball?

ST. JOHN *'tuts'*.

BALL (*amazed*). Itch, Sir?

MORN. For power.

Nothing from BALL.

You and the English Army. A blazing, beautiful itch, singing away in a private place. Delicious. That you're not scratching. Yet. You're saving it up. For the day you give in, throw all caution, all self-respect, all decency and discipline of your trade . . . To the winds. And rip off your glove. And scratch. (*He bares his teeth and growls into* BALL'*s face.*)

Nothing from BALL.

So the blood flows, eh? And you tear the skin back, eh? Rip the flesh. And you go on, through the epidermic wall, deep into the body, to put your hand on an internal organ, liver, kidney, heart . . . To squeeze. I speak of the body politic.

BALL. I see, Sir.

MORN. The English Army taking over England.

BALL. I'm a professional, sir.

MORN. Phooey.

ST. JOHN. Gerald.

The SOLDIER *comes on, with the tray replenished with drinks.*

MORN (*he moves away from* BALL *with a shrug*). We are all caught up in some vast conspiracy of obedience. Who is responsible? None of us, all of us.

The SOLDIER *with the drinks reaches him. He takes a glass, downs it.*

BALL (*angry*). Yes. Please do top up.

MORN *puts the drink down and takes another. He wanders away.*

ST. JOHN (*confidentially to* BALL). Please take no offence at Mr Morn. My colleague from the House is often tired.

BALL. I see, Sir.

ST. JOHN. Tired, you understand.

MORN *goes right up to* SERGEANT BAXTER, *breathing alcohol into his face.*

MORN. What do you feel?

SERGEANT. 'Feel' Sir?

MORN. About the men's recreation.

SERGEANT. Personally Sir?

MORN. Why not?

SERGEANT. Personally. (*Eyeball to eyeball with* MORN *now.*) Put it like this, Sir. What do you do with a slobbering, rabid dog? Don't let it go round infecting us all, do you Sir? Y' take it out and shoot it, don't you Sir? Like we did in Ireland.

MORN. Yesh. (*Caught in the* SERGEANT'*s stare.*) Yeah.

SERGEANT. Perhaps you should sit down, Sir, if you don't feel too well.

MORN *turns away and replenishes his glass from a hip flask.*

ST JOHN (*turns to* JULIA). Perhaps you should have a word with Gerald, Julia.

JULIA. I am not a nurse to this Committee.

BALL. Let's get this over with, Thompson.

THOMPSON. Yes, Sir. (*Publicly.*) Ladies and Gentlemen, could I have your attention please. Ladies and Gentlemen.

They quieten.

The entertainment prepared by the men of Churchill . . . Is about to begin. So I . . . If . . . If you could take your seats.

They do so, chattering.

JULIA. How was this entertainment made, Colonel?

BALL. One for you I think, Captain Thompson.

THOMPSON. Thank you, Sir. The men devised the entertainment themselves, making their own speeches. They made the costumes and the props. It is their own expression.

GLENDA. Very jolly. (*Nods and smiles.*)

JULIA. Quixotic.

BALL *shakes his head at* GLENDA.

ST. JOHN. They are literate.

THOMPSON (*a slight pause*). Why should they *not* be literate, sir?

ST. JOHN. What?

THOMPSON. Why they should not . . . Be.

ST. JOHN. There is a rate of illiteracy in the country . . .

THOMPSON. It is not solely among the working classes, Sir.

ST. JOHN. No? No, of course not. I remember at my school, there were nincompoops. I suppose there are civil servants still on Enid Blyton somewhere.

THOMPSON *doesn't laugh.* ST. JOHN *not pleased.*

MORN. So everything. (*A slight pause.*) They say, they mean. Their own sentiments. Of the men.

THOMPSON. Yes, sir.

MORN. And they don't just stand there and scream? (*Spitting.*) Shower us with accusation. Spit. Disapprobation. Eh?

THOMPSON. Sir. (*He turns away, and sits down.*)

MORN (*ignored by all*). Oh you sods. You sods.

BALL (*publicly, with a grin*). Hope to God you've cleaned this up, Thompson. Cut out the abuse and the bits about Welsh miners.

THOMPSON. All above board now, Sir.

BALL. How did you manage that? Or should I be deaf and blind.

THOMPSON. Promised the men a perk. Five crates of Guinness, Sir.

BALL. I am deaf and I am blind.

THOMPSON. Thank you, Sir.

> FURRY *steps forward with a dustbin lid. He hits it with a hammer.*

FURRY (*aggressively*). I jus' wanna say this. 'Bout dirty words. When there's a dirty word, in play . . . Stead of yer gerrin' dirty word in yer face, I hit my gong. This (*Brandishing the dustbin lid.*) is my gong. (*He hits the dustbin lid with the hammer.*) Right? Right. Jus' so yer know. An' ladies present won't get their knickers in a twist by foul language. So (*He hits the dustbin lid.*) to you all.

> *Uncertain applause. A silence with occasional coughs.* FURRY *at the little electrical board.*

FURRY. One. Two. Three. Go.

> *Light on the little stage. The Union Jack curtain rises. The 'scene' is the same as that at the beginning of Act One, but the whole presentation is coarser. A dim light. Above, a huge stained glass window of medieval knights in prayer. Below, candles round a huge catafalque which is draped with the Union Jack. At each corner a* SERVICEMAN *stands guard, head lowered in mourning. The parts are played as before.* JACK WILLIAMS *as*

the Marine, TED BARKER *as the Private,* MIKE MCCULLOCH *as the Seaman,* JIMMY UMPLEBY *as the Airman.*

TED. Body of Sir Winston Churchill. And I a poor soldier guarding his remains. My Mum cried when I told her. Loved him, loved him, she cried. My Mum cried. Yes, something to write home about. To say I was there, night they laid him, there in the dark.

MIKE (*aside*). Standing guard you get to thinking. And imagining. The general public come up to you and torment you. Dogs pass. It rains. It sleets. It snows. Sun comes out, sweat runs down your nose. And your mind . . . Drifts. Night jobs like this are worst. Spots before your eyes. Planets. Moons and stars. You fall through the floor. Thinking of your life, and just what the (FURRY *hits the dustbin lid.*) you're doing. And you fall. Toecaps . . . Spats . . . The crease of your uniform slices through the stone. And you fall. Through England.

JIMMY. Hey, mate.

MIKE. Hush.

JIMMY. Oh my Godfather. Mate.

MIKE. What?

JIMMY. Oh Jesus Christ.

MIKE. What is the bloody matter with you?

JIMMY. Don't you hear?

MIKE. Hear what?

JIMMY. Knocking.

MIKE. Knocking?

JIMMY. He knocked.

MIKE. You're one under.

JIMMY. He wants to get out.

TED. Hey, you two. Shut it.

MIKE. Sonny boy, he heard a knock.

TED. Knock?

MIKE. From behind.

A knocking heard from inside the coffin.

TED. A bird, caught under the lid.

A knocking from inside the coffin. CHURCHILL *forces the lid off and sits up, swirled with the flag. He has an unlit cigar.*

JACK. Don't look now, but I think we've got a problem.

They look round.

JIMMY. Back from the dead!
TED. Back from the dead!
JACK. Back from the dead!
MIKE. That's not decent. To come back from the dead like that!

A pause. Whispers.

JACK. That's what he looked like, close up to.
TED. Wait till my Mum hears about this.
JACK. That's what's on the stamps. And the Memorial Five Bob bit in Presentation Case.
TED. Do you think a corpse can sign an autograph?

CHURCHILL, *a massive victory sign with cigar.*

JACK. Victory from the grave. That's what that is, victory from the grave.
JIMMY. I think I've cottoned on. The living dead.
TED. Living dead?
JIMMY. Straight case. Like Dracula, come back for blood and young women's necks. Take a stake through the heart to get him back in the grave. Or a cross. Or a twig of wolfbane. Or sunlight, the first rays of dawn. And there's something else.
TED. Surprise me.
JIMMY. The way you get to being a vampire is by being bit by another vampire. Your blood is . . . Translated.
TED. So?
JIMMY. So, who bit him.
JACK. Evens on General de Gaulle.
JIMMY. Maybe they're all the living dead. All the leaders of the

world. Vampires. Imagine them in the Gents Toilet at the United Nations, sucking each other's necks.

CHURCHILL *yawns and stretches, then beckons to* SERVICE-MEN.

TED. Don't like the look of that. I'm off.

JIMMY. Too right.

JACK. Me too.

TED. Guarding the remains of a great man is one thing, and all very well. But when he sits up and waves at you . . . No thank you.

JIMMY. First ray of the sun through the window, that'll see him off.

JACK. Dying for a fag just to calm my nerves.

JIMMY. Right.

TED. Right.

JACK. Coming, mate?

MIKE. I'll stay on here.

JACK. What, with that?

MIKE. I've got a bone to pick with him.

JACK. You? A bone to pick with that?

JIMMY. You got a bone to pick with Sir Winston (*The dustbin struck.*) Churchill?

TED. What can a scabby jock layabout like you have to pick over with the Man who Won the Second World War?

MIKE. I've got a (*Dustbin lid.*) bone to (*Dustbin lid.*) pick over here, so (*Dustbin lid.*) off.

A drum roll from FURRY, *on the dustbin lid.* JIMMY, TED *and* JACK *turn and shrug to the audience and go off.*

Eh. You. Mister.

CHURCHILL. Jack Tar. Give us a light, jolly Jack Tar.

MIKE *gives* CHURCHILL *a light.* CHURCHILL *smokes.*

Where am I?

MIKE. At your funeral.

CHURCHILL. Shovelling me away are they, after all these years?

MIKE. Shovelling you away.

CHURCHILL. Won't go! Won't! Won't, even now, let go.

MIKE. Want to be Prime Minister again?

CHURCHILL. Why not?

MIKE. You're dead, that's why not.

CHURCHILL. That has not stopped others.

MIKE. Britain ruled by a corpse?

CHURCHILL. I'm a fresh corpse. Fresh yet. And the smell is healthy. Juicy. Of the earth, England's earth. The country will get used to it. They were always fond of me. I always felt love rising to me from English crowds, sweet, sticky affection. Like your town.

MIKE. My town?

CHURCHILL. Glasgow lad, aren't you?

MIKE. I may be.

CHURCHILL. A grey, overcast day. The June of 1945. Spoke in the open air. Boys perched in the trees. Men stood in serried ranks on the roofs, round about. Wonderful sight. The beauty of so many human faces lit in a flash with welcome and joy. Young women whose beauty charmed the eye, old ladies brought out in chairs, or waved flags from windows. Dazzled me. When I had said my few words they sang 'Will Ye No Come Back Agin'. Glasgow dazzled me.

MIKE. Dazzled you? Glasgow? Old man you don't know the half. Clydebank, my father was born. Thirteenth of March, 1941. Night of the first great German raid on the town. We walked out, my father hours old in Gran'ma's arms, and she in a cart they had in the buildings for coal, a midwife with us from over the way. We walked out of the town. Out to the moors. Some stayed for weeks, camped out in the open air. My father's first night alive was on the moors. And the next night, fourteenth of March, came the second great air raid. Of twelve thousand dwellings, seven only hit. Of forty-seven thousand souls, thirty-five thousand homeless. From that time on, for many months, but for a few, the whole population went to the moor at night. Me Grand'ma described the scene. The camp fires, the cooking in the little valleys and hollows of the lowland hills. The poor, from the bombed city, under the stars, hey?

CHURCHILL. The lights went out and the bombs came down. Out of the jaws of death.

MIKE. Old man, we don't live in the same world.

CHURCHILL. It's not all ermine robes to wipe your bottom where I come from.

MIKE. Nor is it all cloth caps and waving flags where I come from.

CHURCHILL. We're both of the Island Race. Out of the Celtic mist. The Saxon fen. And bitter, dark green Normandy.

MIKE. I did not understand a word of that.

CHURCHILL. Blood. Heritage . . . (*He clutches his heart.*) Pain.

MIKE. What's the matter?

CHURCHILL. Bowels of the earth.

MIKE. You what?

CHURCHILL. Pain. Help me out of this damn contraption. This engine for dead war heroes.

MIKE *helps* CHURCHILL *out of the catafalque.*

MIKE. Don't like to touch you. You may fall apart. In my hands. Bits a Sir Winston Churchill. I don't fancy that.

CHURCHILL. Don't be squeamish. First World War, saw bits of men in the trenches, shovelled into bags with mud and wet stone, the pink against the brown, to be blessed by the Chaplain. We're all meat, laddy. Lit momentarily by the divine spark. Or whatever it is makes us plough so brutally through life.

CHURCHILL *is out of the coffin. He leans on* MIKE'*s arm.*

MIKE. Your foot looks bad.

CHURCHILL. It's falling off.

CHURCHILL *nearly falls*. MIKE *cradles him*.

Your eyes are blue, Jack Tar.

MIKE. Yours are kind of pus-coloured.

CHURCHILL. I'm a dying bit of Old England, Jack Tar. (*Scared*.) What's in the corner . . .?

MIKE. Nothing is in the corner.

CHURCHILL. A black dog?

MIKE. Churchill, you left us nothing. Few statues of you, in your boiler suit. Your name in a kid's skipping rhyme. Adventure story from some lost, colonial war. Bit a gas from our fathers about some darkest hour years ago. Gas only, not a single human thought. Not a single true, human remain.

CHURCHILL. Words! Words! Left you words! Listen, listen. I'm speaking to you from the grave. My words, hammered out. Sh.

MIKE (*aside*). A one two three, a rave from the grave.

FURRY *gives a drum roll on the dustbin lid*.

JOBY (*at once the* CHURCHILL *manner dropped completely. To the* SELECT COMMITTEE). I just like t'put a word in 'ere. Speakin' as a man now, who's goin' t' do Blood, Sweat an' Tears speech up 'ere . . .

MIKE (*to himself*). Ah Joby, just get on wi' it.

JOBY. I'd jus' like t'say . . . (*Slight pause*.) This dead, great old man I'm tryin' t'put before ye. Fer a few laughs. I'd like t'put this in 'play with special feelin'.

MIKE (*to himself*). Joby, you old clot.

JOBY. Alright, I know me own mind. (*A pause*.) Gerron wi' it, then.

MIKE (*back in the play*). . . . Rave from the grave.

FURRY *gives a drum roll on the dustbin lid*.

CHURCHILL (JOBY *composes himself, then*). In this crisis I hope I may be pardoned if I do not address the House at any length today. I would say to the House . . . 'I have nothing to offer but blood, toil, tears and sweat.' We have before us an ordeal of the most grievous kind. We have before us many, many long months of struggle and of suffering. You ask what is our policy? I will say: It is to wage war, by sea, land and air, with all our might and with all the strength that God can give us; to wage war against a monstrous tyranny, never surpassed in the dark, lamentable catalogue of human crime. That is our policy. You ask, what is our aim? I can answer that in one word – Victory, victory at all costs, victory in spite of all terror, victory, however long and hard the road may be; for without victory, there is no survival. Let that be realized; no survival for the British Empire; no survival for all that the British Empire has stood for, no survival for the urge and impulse of the ages that mankind will move forward towards its goal. But I take up my task with buoyancy and hope. I feel sure that our case will not be suffered to fail amongst men. At this time I feel entitled to claim the aid of all, and I say, 'Come, then, let us go forward together with our united strength'.

A dog howls from behind the little stage.

Black Dog! Throw something at it, quick, before it gets me. Dogs dig up dead men.

FURRY *lets the Union Jack curtain down then shambles onto the stage. He carries a piece of paper. He drops it.*

FURRY. Dropped it. (*He stoops. Picks up the paper. Reads.*) An 'istorical note. Sir Winston Churchill 'ad terrible fits a depression. He called these fits, Black Dog. When 'e 'ad the fit come on, 'e would cancel all appointments, and shut 'imself up. Not even Mrs Churchill could come into 'room, when Black Dog was upon 'im. So. (*He looks up.*) That's what's goin' on. (*He shambles off and pulls the Union Jack curtain up.*)

BLACK DOG, *played by* PETER REESE, *stands at* CHURCHILL'*s side. A shaggy, mangy dog.*

BLACK DOG. Woof! Winston, I'm still with you.

CHURCHILL. Black Dog . . . The very night London burned, the second great fire . . . I saw you, bounding along, among the fire hoses beneath St. Paul's.

BLACK DOG (*pants*). Tell it to us, Winston. (*Pants.*)

CHURCHILL. Childhood? Hedged by fears. As a young boy in the great Blenheim Palace Library, little Winston Churchill, me, took down the dark books of the Spanish Inquisition. Read of the whips, the racks, the brands.

BLACK DOG *howls.*

Naked body on the wheel, over the fire. Naked young monks at the side of the Saint, laid on the red hot irons of the griddle . . .

BLACK DOG *howls.*

Up in my room, high in the dark Palace of the Marlboroughs, my toy battlefield went for miles over the carpet. The carnage of leaden severed heads, little leaden groins filled my imagination with terror. I was a sad little boy. Nine years old, brutally put to prep. school. The English Public School system is there for the brutalization of the Ruling Classes, not their benefit. And Harrow is an abattoir to hack out the sensitive spirit, the all too human meat of the shy, fat boy. Dogged. Dogged. (*He points at* BLACK DOG.)

BLACK DOG. His-tory. Fam-ily. Privil-ege. Duuuuu-ty. (*He howls.*)

CHURCHILL. A little shift of history . . . And I would be remembered as a minor English impressionist painter.

BLACK DOG. His-toreeeeee . . . (*Pants.*) His daddy, his daddy . . .

CHURCHILL. Throw something at it, break its legs.

BLACK DOG *snarls and crouches.*

Of my father's syphilis. The tender secret my family has cherished, the terrible fact. Lord Randolph Churchill, brilliant meteor of his day, the man they said would run the English Twentieth Century . . . Died of that filthy disease . . . I came home from India, to a quiet sitting-room. Out of the window the English countryside and warm, gentle rain. By the fireside, my father. An English aristocrat, fine, arrogant. The honed grace of his class, ground and polished. The natural right of an English gentleman to rule . . . For there was a quality of History about him . . . Shone about his very features. (*A pause.*) I cannot express, even to myself, the obscenity of what the disease had done to him. It had . . . Scraped his brain. Despite the heavy cologne his nurses doused upon him, he smelt. His affections had putrefied. All his sense was of self-pity. One yearned, like one yearns for love, for a coherent remark. One scanned his dribble for a sign. For him to say, merely . . . It is the disease, it is the disease. But he was gentle. lost in the vile, infected marsh of his illness. A marsh light. (BLACK DOG *whimpers.*) I have feared his disease all my life. When Black Dog came, thought . . . This is it! My Father's disease, visited upon me, as the Bible says, generation upon generation . . . In the lavatory would look at myself for chancres, little signs, eczemas, rashes, the slightest inflamed pimple . . . Made me mad with fear! The bridge of my nose! On the rot! Spent hours before mirrors. Should it ever come upon me, I resolved, I would kill myself. Took that resolve into the grave. Won't read that in the official biography.

FURRY *comes on. He speaks aside to the official audience.*

FURRY. Change a whar the scene's at, 'ere. (*He pulls a cord. A white sheet comes down. On it is the legend. 'We can take it, Guv. Give it 'em back'.*) An' I'm goin' t'nip round back, 'cos I'm goin' t'do a bit a actin' in a jiffy. See yer, right? Right.

He gives a thumb-up sign, winks and goes off.

MIKE. Dog, take us back to 1940.
BLACK DOG. On my back, on my back.

CHURCHILL *and* MIKE *get on the back of the dog.*

CHURCHILL. Back through England!

*Through the cloth, slides of post-war English history in reverse,
starting with Churchill's funeral, the catafalque itself. Then the
first Wilson government. William Douglas-Home. Macmillan.
Profumo. Gaitskell. Eden. Suez. Eoka on a Cyprus wall.
Churchill, early fifties. Attlee. Rationing. Bevan. Coal fields
nationalized. Election 1945. Potsdam Conference with Truman.
Yalta Conference with Roosevelt. Berlin bombed. Normandy
invasion. Alamein. Hitler attacks Russia. Finally the photo-
graph of St. Paul's in the 'Second Great Fire' 29th December
1940.*

*These slides are crudely done, as if with a domestic slide pro-
jector, distorted badly from the side on the cloth, spilling across
the hangar to the far wall. Following exchanges over this.*

Where are we going, lad!
MIKE. Meet my Uncle Ern!
CHURCHILL. Who?
MIKE. Don't you remember me Uncle Ern?
CHURCHILL. Cannot say, with any honesty, I do.
MIKE. You met my Uncle Ern in 1940!
CHURCHILL. Glasgow man?
MIKE. Not my Uncle Ern from Glasgow, my Uncle Ern from
    Liverpool!
CHURCHILL. I know no such Uncle Ern!
MIKE. December 30th, 1940. In the early morning.
CHURCHILL. Morning after . . .
MIKE. Morning after the Second Great Fire of London.
CHURCHILL. Don't remember. Back through the years . . .
MIKE. Peckham.

CHURCHILL. Peckham?

MIKE. You cried.

CHURCHILL. Did I cry?

MIKE. Winston Churchill cried. And an old woman said . . .

BLACK DOG. We can take it, Guv. Give it 'em back.

CHURCHILL. Did I cry?

The St. Paul's slide.

BLACK DOG. Great Fire of London!

The PRISONERS *stage the Great Fire of London. A battery of effects. The fire is staged all over the stage, off the little stage. The roof, the walls of the hangar ablaze. 'The sky over London was glorious, ochre and madder, as though a dozen tropic suns were simultaneously setting round the horizon . . . Everywhere the shells sparkled like Christmas baubles.'* (Evelyn Waugh)

'The aesthetic pleasure which the fires provoked banished all sense of fear.' (Charlotte Haldene)

Also note : A raid began with parachute flares in clusters, amber or green, casting sharp shadows. Incendiaries were dropped in 'carpets'. They hissed and sparkled with a whitish-green glare.

The white street with the legend rises. Peckham. Early morning. By the edge of a crater. 'What strikes me so forcibly is the tawdry look, the cheap and nasty look this sort of thing wears after the explosion . . . So often it exposes, or seems to, that everything is jerry-built – makes it seem so even if it wasn't. One is humiliated by it.' (J. L. Hodson)

Far at the back there is a mound of rubble and smashed-up furnishings. Uncle Ernie, played by FURRY *and his sister Annie, played by* JIMMY. *Uncle Ernie is in pyjamas, mackintosh, slippers, scarf and coat.* ANNIE *is in dressing gown, hard shoes but no stockings, on her head a scarf turbanned over curlers.* ERNIE *and* ANNIE *are hand in hand.*

MIKE *and* CHURCHILL *dismount from* BLACK DOG, *who retreats, backwards, into the wings of the little stage.*

CHURCHILL. Remember. Peckham landmine. Heard the bang in Ten Downing Street. Drove over to see what was cooking. And I saw these good people, at the side of the crater. And they cried out to me . . .

ERNIE *and* ANNIE *very cheerfully.*

ANNIE. Look. He's crying for us.
ERNIE. Good old Winnie.
ANNIE. We thought you'd come and see us.
ERNIE. We can take it.
ANNIE. Give it 'em back.

They wave, doll-like.

CHURCHILL. And I wept. Deeply moved.
MIKE. Not like my Uncle Ern told me it.
ERNIE. Yer dead right. That were 'myth. This is like it was.

He sags, sits down in the rubble. ANNIE *scuttles back to the rubble.* CHURCHILL *goes off.* ANNIE *scrabbles in the rubble, she finds a dinner-table chair. She puts it at the front of the stage. This way, going back and forth out the dust and wreckage, she assembles a dinner-table suite and living-room. The table has two legs and is splintered. Three chairs, none of which stands. The charred remains of an easy chair. The delicate shell of a smashed china display cabinet, glass-fronted, all the glass gone. She finds pieces of glass and china, unrecognizable lumps, and carefully puts them in the cabinet. Then she sits on the ground, in the middle of the 'room' salvaged from her home.*

Wish you would not. (*A pause.*) Wish you would not, Annie.

A gentle, shocked gesture from her.

(*Aside.*) And he walked up.

CHURCHILL *comes on. He is in an overcoat, with Homburg and walking stick. He looks at* ERNIE.

Sir Winston Churchill. Just there. Oh aye, I thought, looking across. (*He looks across.*) Oh aye. I'll say this – he looked well. But then they do, don't they. Pay clerks upwards, they all look well. Difference between steak and mucky sausages, true meat and mashed up lung. Tells, in the end. Aye, I looked across. At the myth. Standing there. Like he'd come down from a cinema screen, out of a film show. Winnie. With a cigar. And I felt angry, suddenly, angry. Sat there with me life. Which is to do with being widowed and having a dicky lung. And coming to London to live with me sister Annie. For light work, you see. And getting it in a warehouse, Morleys gents outfitters, but the warehouse going early on in a daylight raid . . . Y'know. Your life. And it were sick kind a anger . . . Like water, mixed up with oil. Queasy. And I wanted to say . . . Go away from this hole that were my sister Annie's house. We're alright, we'll come through, what else is there for us. Just go away from this hole. And I made a gesture like this. (*A wave.*)

CHURCHILL *raises his hand in salute.*

And he waved back. And I said, I swear to this day I said . . . Thought you'd come and see us. (*Aside.*) This were like it really were, unzip yer ear'oles . . . (*A slight pause.*) Thought you'd come and see us.

CHURCHILL. Ah. Ah.

ERNIE. We can take it.

CHURCHILL. Ah.

ERNIE. But we just might give it back to you one day.

MIKE. We just might give it back to you one day.

ERNIE. And in his book on war he wrote it down as . . . Give it 'em back.

BLACK DOG. Give it 'em back. (*Howls.*)

MIKE (*aside*). And my old Uncle Ern, in his cups, telling it for the ten thousandth, three hundred and eighty-fourth time.

ERNIE. God rot great men.

MIKE. God rot great men.

BLACK DOG. God rot great men.

CHURCHILL (*raises his stick in a fury*). Who won the war?

ERNIE. Don't you know that? I did. And she did. People won the war.

CHURCHILL sags.

CHURCHILL. God bless you all. God bless you all.

ERNIE. And rot you, too.

The Union Jack curtain tumbles down at once on the little stage.

A silence.

GLENDA. Well, that's done.

A silence.

MORN. Yes.

GLENDA. Did Lord Randolph real . . .

ST. JOHN (*hard*). Yes.

MORN (*unconnected*). Yes . . .

GLENDA. How terrible for the family.

BALL (*aside to* THOMPSON). Five crates of Guinness? For that? (*Turning to* ST. JOHN.)

ST. JOHN. Colonel.

BALL. Sir. (*At once to the* SERGEANT.) Sergeant Baxter.

SERGEANT (*intimately*). Suh.

BALL. Look to that behind there.

SERGEANT. Suh.

He leaps nimbly up onto the stage, under the Union Jack curtain.

MORN. I feel ashamed. I feel responsible.

ST. JOHN. Colonel, I do not think the Committee can look very favourably upon this exhibition.

BALL. No, Sir.

MORN. Deep, abiding, personal sorrow.

GLENDA. Are you feeling alright, Mr Morn?

MORN. I did it to 'em, me. (*Tears.*) And can the future be so black.

ST. JOHN. Shut up, Gerald. (*To* BALL.) You should not allow that. If you give vent to repressed emotions (*Gestures at the stage.*) that, you will get mess and abuse.

BALL. Sir.

GLENDA. Perhaps I could get you something? Anadin? (*She puts her hand on his shoulder. He turns away.*)

THOMPSON. If I may say . . .

BALL. You may not. (*To the* COMMITTEE.) Tea, in the Officers' Mess?

JULIA (*angry*). These men have rioted. Stood in picket lines with stones in their hands. Axe handles, to smash the windows of lorries.

ST. JOHN (*he pauses, then smiles*). Tea. (*He stands.*) Felt I was being got at. We all have to water our paranoia these days, eh Gerald?

MORN *shakes his head.*

(*Giving* MORN *a hand up.*) Come on, old son. Take the plunge and stand up.

The situation emulsified.

BALL. Tea. And an extensive discussion.

THOMPSON *moves forward, jerkily, blushing.*

CAROLINE. Oh don't, Julian . . .

MORN *sits down again. Bad temper at once from* BALL *and* ST JOHN.

THOMPSON (*a blurt*). I must make myself clear.

BALL. No you must not, Captain Thompson.

THOMPSON. I cannot let . . .

BALL. Captain Thompson! (*With a gesture throwing something on the ground.*)

ST. JOHN. What is the matter now?

THOMPSON. Conscience. In all conscience I . . .

> *At once the Union Jack curtain goes up, the* SERGEANT *is tied up in an ugly way.* MIKE *has taken his gun, and holds it to his head. The detainees who performed in the play stand round about.* JOBY *sits smoking ignoring what's going on.* JIMMY *is still in drag.*

MIKE. You all play ball with me, I'll play ball wi' you, and na problem. All sweet, all a us gettin' along just fine. The lady, up.

> *All dead still before the stage.*

(*Furious.*) Lady, lady lady M.P, up here now! And watch, watch 'em!

> JIMMY *leaps down and grabs* JULIA.

JULIA. Don't you touch me. (*Swings her handbag.*)

> JIMMY *jumps out of the way.*

MIKE. Don't be rough now, Jimmy. And na screetchin', lady. Step up here. Give her a hand up, Jimmy.

JIMMY. Lady.

> *With an odd bow he gives her a hand up on the stage. She finds herself staring at* JOBY, *who smokes. Then gives a kiss-kiss with his lips.*

MIKE (*moves the gun over at* JULIA's *head very slowly*). We are going to think now, we are going to go moment by moment now.

The SERGEANT, *the gun away from his head, immediately begins to struggle.*

Are we not, Colonel.

BALL. Yes we are, McCulloch.

ST. JOHN *about to say something. The* COLONEL *turns to him calmly.*

BALL. Please be silent and absolutely still, Sir.

MORN *looks up.*

(*To* ST. JOHN.) And Mr Morn please sir.

MIKE. Your arms, and Captain Thompson's arms, Colonel.

The COLONEL *moves his hand.*

No no, we are collecting.

JACK. That slimy bastard is armed. (*Indicates* ST. JOHN.)

FURRY *takes the sidearms from* THOMPSON *and* BALL, *and from the* GUARDS.

MIKE (*to* ST. JOHN, *indicating raise your arms*). You carry a firearm, Sir?

ST. JOHN *does,* FURRY *takes it.*

Now, Colonel Ball, you carry a key to the armoury.

A silence.

You carry a key to the armoury. You do na leave it your office, which is sensible. You carry a key. (*A silence.*) The situation you have. Moment t'moment, now.

BALL *pauses, then takes a key out of a wallet of keys and throws it to* MIKE. MIKE *lets the key fall against him, not looking at it.*

Pick that up for me, Jimmy.

JIMMY (*picks it up*). Key t'Eaven. (*Holds it up.*)

SERGEANT. Get out a hand, Michael.

ST. JOHN. You must consider.

BALL. BE QUIET, Sir.

A silence . . .

MIKE. Up on the chairs.

SERGEANT. Michael . . .

TED (*to* MIKE). You what?

MIKE. Stick 'em up on the chairs.

JIMMY. Yeah! Get 'em up on the chairs! 'Ouse a wax. Y'enemies, in a row.

MIKE. So we can see 'em, Jimmy. That's all. Ladies and gentlemen, would you stand on your chairs. Now please.

FURRY. Better 'ave 'em put their 'ands behind their necks. Like this.

The party hesitate.

ST. JOHN. Atrocity? Upon us? Are you about . . .?

JACK. Stand up on your chairs!

CAROLINE (*whimpers*). No. No.

THOMPSON. In all conscience.

BALL (*shouts at* THOMPSON). Shut up, shut up, shut up, you ill-disciplined, selfish, self-regarding . . .

A pause. All still.

We all stand up on our chairs. Please. Now.

The party stand up on their chairs. MORN *is incapable.*

JACK. And their handbags and things now, right? Ladies, throw down your handbags. The men don't go to your pockets. We'll do that.

TED. We need money. For the journey. And your overcoats – we'll be sleeping rough.

MIKE. Give the drunk a hand.

FURRY (*to* MORN). Eh up.

MORN. Obsol . . . es . . . cent.

FURRY. Y'got to stand up now. On y'chair.

MORN. My day. Done. Utterly spent. I believed in . . . (*He shrugs.*) Now. (*Tears.*) I'm a drunk and . . . (*He looks up.*) You've got guns.

> FURRY *takes* MORN's *flask and cigarettes.* JIMMY *rummages in the women's handbags. He takes a photograph from* CAROLINE.

JIMMY. Who's the old lady, y'Mum?

JULIA. Don't touch our things. Don't put your fingers on our things.

JIMMY. Picture of an 'ouse.

> JIMMY *pockets a purse, then takes out lipstick and mirror, throws the handbag away and begins to make up.*

SERGEANT. You'll be all over the tarmac, Michael. You'll not reach the wire, know that? You will be a slime on the tarmac.

CAROLINE (*at* JIMMY). A house. Why do you sneer at that? (*At* THOMPSON.) Why do you sneer at that? (*And* at JIMMY.) Not wrong to want that. In peace. Grow the vegetables. Recycle. Save the heat of your own body. Sunlight for power. A glass roof, and plants growing, under the eaves. Yes. And children in bright clothes. On the swing. On the lawn. That's what I want. That's not obscene, is it? The house. The lawn. The plants. The children playing . . . That's not obscene . . .

JIMMY. Want a house do you, Lady? What, with a garden? Yeah, and barbed wire round t'stop dirty animals like me getting in? Oh Lady, Neo-luddites'll come out a the dark. Right through plate glass window of your house. Kick in your three-D colour telly. And paraffin on your fancy furniture. And burn you, burn you bright.

CAROLINE. What have I ever?

JIMMY. Ever? Ever? What, ever done?

TED. Jimmy, cut it out.

CAROLINE. What have I ever done to you?

JIMMY. You put me in 'ere, Lady. (*To* MIKE.) She put me in 'ere. (*Shouts at her.*) Lady!

MIKE. Now, Jimmy, go carefully.

> JIMMY *runs about the hangar shouting.* TED *and* JACK *run after him.*

JIMMY. Burn. Burn. You got to burn. Set alight.

SERGEANT. . . . Michael, out a your hands!

CORPORAL. . . . You'll kill yourselves!

> JIMMY *fires the Sten gun offstage. He comes back on.*

JIMMY (*quietly*). I fired through the wall at 'em. I fired through the wall.

> *A silence. All dead still.*

MIKE. Jack. Go and look on the outside.

JACK. Right.

> JACK *runs up and down the hangar's wall, looking out of cracks.*

REESE. You had better give me that.

> JIMMY *gives* REESE *the gun.*

SERGEANT. And now they will burn you, Michael.

MICHAEL. Not with the ladies and gentlemen.

SERGEANT. Oh Michael, Michael. They will come in 'ere and burn everything in sight!

> *A silence.*

What you gonna do? Walk out with hostages? Into the sunset and happy ever after? They'd not let you lot out, spewed all over the countryside, armed. Running in the woods? Into people's back gardens?

GLENDA (*quietly*). I don't want the future to be like this.

CORPORAL. Jack? Ted? Furry? You stay in 'ere, where they put you. Got a new football for you. Yeah, you just stay in 'ere. Out there . . . (*He shakes his head.*)

ST. JOHN. Shoot civilians? Colonel, your command?

BALL (*slowly getting off the chair*). The huts. Always sinking. The damp. The men . . . Rotting.

The men start but don't move at him.

JULIA. You know what cancer cells are? That's what you are.

JACK comes downstage.

JOBY. I never noticed. (*As* CHURCHILL.) Cancer cells? We will fight them on the beaches . . . (*He gives a V-sign.*)

JACK. They're out there. In their glory. And we are tight now, in this tin can. (*A slight pause.*) Mike, they have searchlights.

MIKE (*bangs the stage hard*). Right. Right. Get down.

The people on the chairs hesitate.

You sit, and you sit, and you sit. (*To* JULIA.) And you stay right there now, wi' Sir Winston Churchill.

JOBY. Never noticed. Ten years, the country sliding down. Through the nineteen seventies. Guns. Barbed wire. The woods stripped clean a their leaves. Journalist I were. Good story that. But I never noticed.

JACK. Old men's bloody stories. I say we still go out.

TED. We make demands. Bargain.

JACK. No we go! We go!

THOMPSON stands.

THOMPSON. Look.

JACK. At what?

THOMPSON. I . . .

JACK. You?

THOMPSON. Doctor. Come with you.

JACK. You?

THOMPSON. I'm a doctor. You'll have to cross country. Have wounds.

CAROLINE (*uncomprehending*). Julian?

THOMPSON. House, lawn, plants under the roof. All built on this. Mud, these men. (*A slight pause. To the men.*) I am a doctor.

They turn from him.

JACK. We go.

JIMMY. What else is there for us, you see? Go out, on fire. Wi' a gesture. Roman candle, a million sparks. Eh? (*He looks round the group.*) Eh?

FURRY. We're like the plague. They'll not let us out of 'ere.

JIMMY. Joby?

JOBY (*taking the mask off*). Dunno. You left me behind, lads. Na, I belong to another world.

JIMMY. Mike?

A pause.

MIKE. I don't know. Break out we thought. Freedom we thought. Get to a big city, lose ourselves among the people. Go to the hills. Or only . . . Reach the sea, eh? Be on a beach in winter. Clean, in the clean air. Joby, Ted, Furry, Jimmy, Jack, Peter. We turn the guns in.

JIMMY. No . . .

JACK. . . . No! That's not human!

MIKE. What's human? Here we find ourselves. And we go out that door, and they cut us down, and Joby, Ted, Furry, Jimmy, Jack, Peter, Mike are shredded meat. Hanging on the wire for the birds . . . That 'Human'? (*A pause.*) Nowhere to break out to, is there. They'll concrete the whole world over any moment now. And what do we do? (*A slight pause. Smiles.*) Survive. In the cracks. Either side of the wire. Be alive.

REESE. Lower than the lowest.

They look at REESE.

MIKE. Yes what do you say, Peter Reese?
REESE. I say . . .

At once the lights go out.

TED (*shouts*). They cut the lights.

At once matches flare.

JACK. Get light, get light.
GLENDA. Don't let the future . . .

A great deep clang. The doors are opening. Outside the revving engines of motor bikes. Blinding light from searchlights. Loudspeakers all round the hangar call out.

LOUDSPEAKERS. PEAKE. BARKER. KEEGAN. UMPLEBY. WILLIAMS. REESE. MCCULLOCH. PEAKE. BARKER. KEEGAN. UMPLEBY. WILLIAMS. REESE. MCCULLOCH . . .

The curtain falls slowly, the PRISONERS *standing in the searchlights.*

Methuen's Modern Plays

EDITED BY JOHN CULLEN and GEOFFREY STRACHAN

Methuen's Theatre Classics